EATING
WILD
PLANTS

EATING
WILD
PLANTS

Kim Williams

Illustrations are by the author.

Mountain Press Publishing Co.
279 West Front Street
Missoula, Montana 59801

Library of Congress Cataloging in Publication Data

Williams, Kim.
    Eating wild plants.

    Bibliography: p.
    Includes index.
      1. Wild plants, Edible.   2. Poisonous plants.
I. Title.
QK98.5.A1W54   581.6'32   76-17916
ISBN 0-87842-065-7

Introduction

Here is a delightful book about wild foods that tells you exactly what you want to know about salad greens, potherbs, roots, fruits, berries, herb teas and mushrooms — plus a chapter on poisonous plants.

The author has a solid background in both nutrition and botany, starting with a BS degree from Cornell University, and combining study and field trips from the Atlantic to the Pacific and even the Andes Mountains of South America.

At present Mrs. Williams teaches a course called "Edible Wild Foods" at the University of Montana and writes free-lance articles for newspapers and magazines.

Mrs. Williams enjoys using edible wild plants and she includes her own experiences. She takes her subject seriously but writes with a light touch. This book can be read for pure enjoyment as well as for solid information.

The book is an introduction to nature that says nature will take care of people if people take care of nature.

"Don't go through the outdoors like Attila the Hun," Kim Williams says. "Take only a little but enjoy the taking."

Dr. Sherman J. Preece, Jr.
Chairman
Department of Botany
University of Montana
Missoula, Mt.

Acknowledgments

I am including a selected bibliography but I have studied edible wild plants all my life and I could not begin to list all my sources. I wish to thank all the people who have studied and written about this subject and have passed the information down the line.

I also wish to state that I have included a great deal of forklore. This has also been passed down the line from person to person, from writer to writer, and perhaps the truth was never there in the first place.

But what would a book about edible wild plants be without its fascinating folklore background? I certainly can't omit that the common plantain "held firmly in the left hand" was the magic talisman that made Alexander the Great so great. You know it isn't true and I know it isn't true but isn't it a marvelous tidbit to muse over on a winter night?

Some of this material has appeared in *The Missoulian*,
in columns written by the author.

Contents

Selected Bibliography

Angier, Bradford. 1972. *Feasting Free on Wild Edibles.* Stackpole Books, Harrisburg, Pa.

Berglund, Berndt and Bolsby, Clare E. 1971. *The Edible Wild.* Charles Scribner's Sons, New York, N.Y.

Brown, Annora. 1954. *Old Man's Garden.* J.M. Dent & Sons, Ltd. Canada, Toronto-Vancouver.

Craighead, John J. and Frank C., and Davis, Ray J. 1963. *A Field Guide to Rocky Mountain Wildflowers.* Houghton Mifflin Company, Boston, Ma.

Gibbons, Euell. 1970. *Stalking the Wild Asparagus.* David McKay Company, Inc. New York.

Harrington, H.D. 1972. *Western Edible Wild Plants.* University of New Mexico Press, Albuquerque, N.M.

Hitchcock, Charles Leo and Cronquist, Arthur. 1973. *Flora of the Pacific Northwest.* University of Washington Press, Seattle and London.

Kingsbury, John M. 1964. *Poisonous Plants of the United States and Canada.* Prentice-Hall, Inc., Engelwood Cliffs, N.J.

EATING WILD PLANTS

This is a book to read and enjoy.
When spring puts out its green
feelers you can put this book in
your pocket and hike into the
hills — to identify plants, to eat
some and to marvel at many.

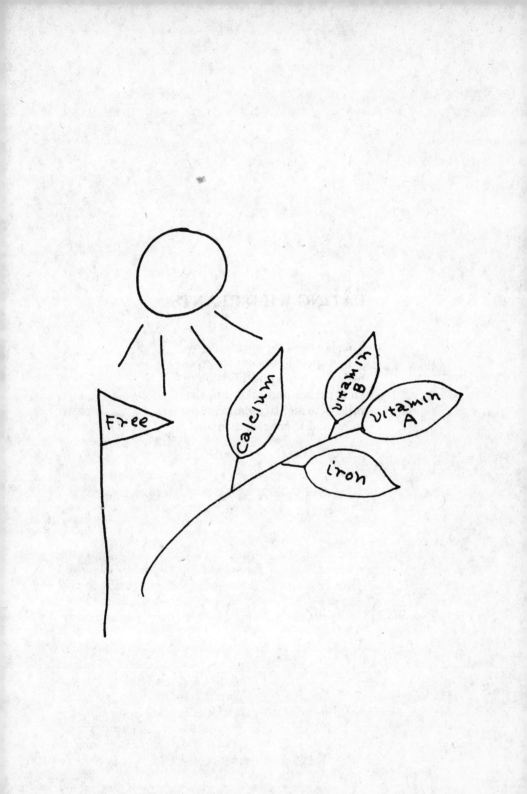

Why Eat Wild Plants?

Why should a person eat wild plants when the stores are full of fruits and vegetables?

I have many reasons. The most important is that eating wild plants is a hobby with me. I do not intend to "live off the land" or "live free." Ninety-five per cent of my food comes from stores. But the five per cent I get free from the outdoors is very important to me.

My pleasure in the outdoors is greatly increased by knowing what berry I can pop into my mouth on a hike or which greens I can add to a salad bowl.

Other people must feel the same because books on edible wild plants are in great demand and classes on the subject are booked in advance.

A renewed interest in edible wild foods goes hand in hand with the present day popularity of backpacking and wilderness vacations.

If you know what you can expect to find along the trail, you can carry less on your back.

In an emergency you can survive. In my classes we make up "survival stewpot" recipies for all four seasons. You do not need to starve if you are lost in the wilderness.

At home in the city the knowledge of what plants (you can call them weeds if you like) are edible adds interest to even a stroll to the library. A walk through a park or an alley is an adventure of discovery. Three rose hips for a colorful touch in the stew, nibble on a fruit from a cheeseweed, pick a violet leaf for an herb tea.

Ten Basic Rules for Eating Wild Plants Safely

There are poisonous plants. In learning about edible wild plants, the important thing to know is how to enjoy the edible ones without becoming endangered by the poisonous ones.

I have found the following ten rules helpful.

1.   Do not eat anything that you cannot positively identify. There is no use taking a chance. As I say to my mushroom class, "Why poison yourself for forty cents? You can buy a can of mushrooms in the supermarket for forty cents."

2.   Be prepared to study. There is no shortcut to acquiring the knowledge. You simply have to learn, one by one, which plants are edible and which ones are not. The best way to learn is to have a guide. If you live near someone who eats wild plants and is willing to take you along on his foragings you are fortunate. The next best way is to take a course, preferably one with field trips. The third way to learn is to buy books and study on your own. This way is more work because you have to carefully compare drawings and pictures with the growing plants. You will probably find that several books will be necessary.

3.   Use scientific names. There are too many plants called pigweed, sour grass, chickweed, wild spinach, etc. If you move from one part of the country to another you will find entirely different common names. But the scientific name is one and only. It is the same in Afghanistan as in Montana.

The scientific name consists of two parts, the genus name and the species name. Sometimes it is very important to know both. For instance, poison ivy is *Rhus radicans* and smooth sumac is *Rhus glabra*. This means that both plants are in the *Rhus* (sumac) genus. However, *Rhus radicans* is poisonous and *Rhus glabra* has fruit that can be used to make a lemonade.

2

4. Learn the plant in all stages of growth: first shoots of spring, flowering plants, fruit stage, and sometimes the dry winter stage. Wild asparagus, for instance, can be found in spring if you have gone on winter walks and have seen the past year's withered stalks reaching above the snow.

5. Start with one or two. You cannot hope to learn all the edible wild plants of your area in one season. Perhaps you'll learn the cattail the first year, trying it in all its stages, letting it become an old friend. Serviceberries can be a new acquaintance for mid-summer, in dessert, jelly or syrup. Rose hips can be an introduction to fall. They are easy to identify and can be used in many ways.

You'll want to look up recipes, perhaps starting a scrapbook and adding bits of knowledge as you go along.

6. Know what part of the plant is edible and when it is edible. For instance, the fruit of the elderberry is edible but chewing on green twigs can make you ill. Of course this is the same with cultivated plants. You eat the tuber of the potato plant but you would not think of eating the leaves. Also, you have learned that ripe apples are delicious but green apples can give you a stomachache. It is the same with wild plants.

7. Use recipes. You will get a much more enjoyable introduction to eating wild plants if you try them properly prepared. Dandelion greens can be delicious. They can also be bitter as gall. Water-cress soup can be a gourmet dish. It can also be something you never want to try again. If your notebook is looseleaf you can try out new material and discard what does not satisfy you.

8. Eat just a sample the first time. Our twentieth century stomachs are not accustomed to pioneer foods. If you have been eating white bread, hamburger and peanut butter, you cannot switch overnight to arrowhead tubers and thistle stems. Also, many wild foods have a very pronounced taste. Some are plain bitter, some are very acid, some have a strong odor. We are accustomed to food with a bland taste. Why do most people prefer head lettuce to green leafy lettuce? The green leafy lettuce has more vitamins and minerals but we like the taste of head lettuce. We like cooked peas rather than Brussels sprouts or cabbage.

There is also the matter of personal reaction. Some people can eat anything, others have digestive upsets very easily. Sometimes a food you can generally eat with no ill effects will suddenly cause trouble. A friend of mine became ill after eating a meal of shaggy mane mushrooms, although he had eaten this same kind of mushroom many times. He figures his body chemistry was different or perhaps the composition of the mushrooms in the certain location where he picked them was different.

Some substances build up in your body. You can eat a certain food two

3

Wild foods are free. Everyone likes something free. I do not condone going through the outdoors like Attila the Hun, digging up everything in sight, reaping harvests by the bushel basket. What will the birds and the wild animals live on if we invade their territory and deplete their food supply? But a pint of berries here and there, a quart of chokecherries, a mess of lamb's quarter — nature can spare that.

In a way it is paying homage to nature to gather from the wild. In our organized world with mile-long rows of corn and beans — planted, fertilized, sprayed and harvested by machine — isn't it an appreciation of nature to pick a berry that grew without being planted or watered or fertilized or sprayed? It's almost a miracle that it grew al all. Maybe when I eat something wild I feel I am participating in that miracle.

Finally, I eat wild foods because I feel I am adding nutritive value to my diet. Many wild plants are so rich in vitamins and minerals they could be called a tonic rather than a food. Didn't Hippocrates back in 500 B.C. say "Let your foods be your medicine."? Today we say "You are what you eat."

I like to think the sun-warmed berries are woodsy leaves are putting magic in my cells.

Scientists would call the magic vitamin A, vitamin C, calcium, etc.

The scientists have discovered and named many of these health-giving substances but the process of discovery is still going on. I believe we should eat a wide variety of food. There may be trace elements we don't yet know about.

My budget doesn't include custard apples from the Andes and papayas from Hawaii but water-cress grows in the streams, plantain is in the park, hawthorn fruit hangs over the river.

My foraging hobby will stay with me all my life. It will get me out in spring, keep me out in fall, nourishing my body and my mind.

4

or three days in a row but not four or five.

The tried and true foods we buy in the supermarket have been chosen because on the whole they produce bad effects on very few people. Perhaps a few people cannot eat potatoes but certainly 99 percent can. Most wild plants have been left in the wild because they do not fit into a mass market.

Those of us who eat wild foods do so because we like the idea of enlarging our menu. We like to try different tastes. But we do not make a meal of a food until we have tried just a sample.

9. Watch out for contamination. A plant can be edible but if it is growing at the edge of a field where the farmer has just sprayed, it is not edible. Water-cress should be picked from streams above barnyards and cattle pastures.

10. Know the common poisonous plants of the area. A good question to ask when learning any new plant is, "Is there anything poisonous that looks like this?" You cannot eat wild onions until you know what death-camas looks like. You should not eat meadow mushrooms until you know what the deadly Amanitas look like.

With these ten rules you should be able to venture into the outdoors and come home with something exotic to add to your dinner menu.

I do not advocate trying to live off the land. It is possible and in an emergency it is the only thing to do. It is also fun to try once in a while. One of my students went backpacking for four days and did not touch the food in his pack. Fish and frog legs were the mainstay of his diet but he also ate 18 different wild plants with no ill effects.

But on the whole, we simply cannot do this. With 215,000,000 people in the United States alone, the world is no longer a foraging society. We have to remember that the wild animals and birds depend on wild food while for us it is simply an added pleasure.

Greens are for Salads and Potherbs

Before the era of supermarkets and vitamins in bottles, the first wild greens of spring were not only a treat but a medicine. Sulphur and molasses was the tonic for some families but for others it was a mess of dandelion greens or a salad of water-cress or tea made from fresh strawberry leaves dug from under the snow.

Even today there are parts of the world where wild plants are the only source of vitamin C, the anti-scurvy vitamin. There are also parts where wild plants could be a source but aren't because the knowledge is not there.

My parents did not have a tradition of edible wild plants. Neither did our neighbors or the one-room school we attended. So we did not know that our depression-era diet could have been augmented with vitamins and minerals from nature. Orange juice was expensive but we could have used fresh wild strawberry leaves. Vitamin C is water soluble. We could have poured hot water on strawberry leaves and then drunk the resulting tea.

We could have picked the first dandelion greens, the first violet leaves, the plantain, the chickweed. All these are out long before anything is produced in a garden.

I don't consider the idea of a spring tonic old-fashioned. I like the idea of new spring greens fresh from the earth. And could anything be fresher than dandelion greens ten minutes from earth to salad bowl?

Maybe the hunt for the greens is a tonic also. Don't we have inside of us an age-old greening instinct? We want to be out — to see whether the earth is warming up, to see what is pushing its way through the ground. What better excuse for a Sunday afternoon hike is there than saying, "I have to see if the curly dock is up."

7

Perhaps there will come a time when instead of spraying the new dandelions in our lawn we will rush out and dig them one by one and make a salad for lunch and a potherb for dinner.

Potherb means a green leafy plant cooked like spinach. Herb did not always mean a plant used for seasoning or in folk medicine. Botanically herb means any plant that is not a bush or tree. Herbs have stems that die back to the ground at the end of the growing season. A vegetable is a cultivated herb.

The word vegetable is relatively modern. In the old days what we call vegetables were called simply herbs. A carrot was an herb. So was a beet.

Whether you want to call lamb's quarter a potherb or a cooked vegetable or a "mess of greens" doesn't matter. The important thing is to know that fresh greens are as necessary for us today as they were back in the times when doctors pressed juice out of dandelion crowns to give to run-down patients.

Dandelion

Taraxacum officinale

Our Puritan ancestors wanted the dandelion so badly they brought it from Eugope. We call it a weed and spend a great deal of time drying to dig it out of the lawn.

One definition of a weed is a misplaced flower. Another, this one by Ralph Waldo Emerson, is 'a plant whose virtues have not yet been discovered."

The virtues of dandelion have been discovered but today we think we do not need those virtues. Our ancestors used dandelion as a medicine. The botanical name, *Taraxacum officinale,* means officially recognized as a remedy for internal disorders.

In the days before year-round fresh produce was available, people often fell ill in great numbers during late winter and early spring. Oldtime herb doctors squeezed the juice out of freshly dug dandelion roots and gave it to the sick. They also told the patient to eat the first new leaves as soon as they were out.

If you look at a nutrition chart, you will see that dandelion leaves are extremely rich in vitamin A and fairly rich in vitamin C, calcium and iron. The oldtime doctors did not know the terms vitamins and minerals but they knew that there was something in certain plants that acted as a tonic.

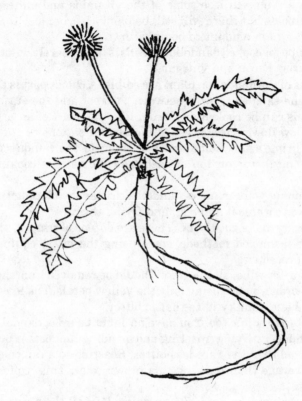

"But dandelion greens are so bitter," you will say. The secret is to pick them in early spring, before the yellow flowers appear. Look for the ones that grow in a shady spot in good soil. I tell my students to pick dandelions under a flatbed truck on the north side of a barn.

If your favorite patch of dandelions is in bright sun, which tends to make them dark green but very bitter, you could blanch them, just as growers used to do with celery. The principle is to keep out the sun so you cover the plants with pots or straw or canvas. Then you will have whitish leaves like the inside part of endive, which is less bitter than the dark green outer part.

Young dandelion leaves can be used raw in a tossed salad or they can be chopped up and added to potato salad, egg salad, creamed tuna, creamed celery, omelet, soups, stews.

If the leaves are too bitter for your taste, try them cooked as a potherb. Some people change the cooking water two or three times to get rid of the bitter taste. You will lose some of the vitamins and minerals in the cooking process but there will still be plenty left because these greens have such a high amount to begin with.

One recipe for cooked dandelion greens is to just barely wilt the greens and add crisp bacon and vinegar.

All parts of the dandelion plant are edible. A choice part is the crown, which is the tangled growth between the root and the surface green leaves. This can be cooked and eaten like the heart of an artichoke.

The yellow flowers are sweet to the taste. I eat one or two on every outing. I bring a few home and add them to the Sunday pancakes, dropping one flower on top of each pancake as it is cooking on the griddle.

Out camping you can make dandelion fritters by dipping the flowers in batter, or cornmeal and egg, and frying them.

The flowers make good wine. There are dozens of recipes, some using simple old-fashioned methods, some using the latest equipment and scientific procedures.

For a sweeter wine, all the green should be removed from the flowers. In other words, you are using only the yellow petals. The leaves, stems and roots have a milky juice that is bitter.

The roots are edible too. You have no doubt heard of dandelion coffee which is made by drying, roasting and grinding the roots. You can peel the roots and then they are less bitter. Roasting to a tan color gives a milder beverage than roasting to a brown color. This "coffee" has no caffeine.

Young roots can be used like parsnips. Parboil them and then fry.

You can have your own supply of tender dandelion greens for winter if you dig up a few plants in fall, pot them with good dirt and place them in your basement. New young leaves will sprout. Due to the absence of sun, the leaves will be blanched. Of course the vitamin content will be less than the dark green sun-grown ones but considering how very rich dandelion greens are in vitamins even basement-grown leaves will be richer than many vegetables we buy in stores. Head lettuce for instance has practically no vitamins or minerals.

Dandelion is generally called a spring green but it can also be a fall green. After the first freeze, you will find new young leaves coming from the crown and these are tender and not too bitter.

Before you pick any wild greens, be sure no one has sprayed in that area with weed-killer.

Water-cress

Rorippa nasturtium-aquaticum

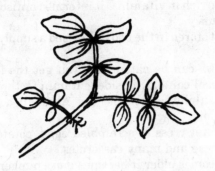

Everyone has heard of water-cress sandwiches but how many of us have eaten them? Water-cress is a vitamin-rich green plant widely used in other parts of the world.

It was brought to the New World long ago and is now well established, growing wild in streams or cultivated for market use.

It is a member of the *Cruciferae* (mustard) family and if you have eaten it you know it has a "bite." One of the common names is pepperleaf.

You have to be careful where you pick this plant. Be sure the water is not contaminated, either by waste water, farm animals or sprays.

Water-cress usually grows in running water, partly submerged and partly floating, but sometimes you find it at the edge of a spring.

The leaves are glossy, dark green, and somewhat fleshy. They are divided into three to nine leaflets. The ribbed stems are hollow. Fine white roots appear at the notes, ready to anchor a new plant and start it growing.

The flowers are four-petaled, white, and not very noticeable.

The poisonous water-hemlock sometimes grows near water-cress. It would be a good idea to check with an expert before eating your first find of cress.

The scientific name is *Rorippa nasturtium-aquaticum*. Nasturtium means "nose twister," referring to the pungent oil in the plant.

The plant has been known since ancient times and used as both a food and medicine. There is an old Greek proverb, "Eat cress and learn more

11

wit." It was believed water-cress could help people whose mind was disturbed.

No doubt most of the help came from the vitamins and minerals in the plant. Since many vitamins are lost very quickly in stored food, a plant like water-cress which could be rushed from stream to salad bowl would be a godsend in pre-refrigerator days.

Water-cress is so rich in vitamin C it is termed antiscorbutic, meaning it will prevent scurvy.

Vitamin C is not stored in the body. We need a supply in our diet every day.

Since water-cress can be eaten raw, you get the full benefit of its vitamin and mineral content. Besides vitamin C, there is A, B and E, and also calcium, sulphur and potassium. All in all, a water-cress salad is a real spring tonic.

You can add water-cress to scrambled eggs, potato salad, creamed soups, cottage cheese and many casseroles.

As the plant becomes older it becomes more pungent and you might prefer to use it as a potherb.

Boiling greens in a small amount of water for as short a time as possible conserves the most vitamins and minerals. If the cooking water is not too bitter you can add it to soup or gravy, thus using the vitamins and minerals dissolved out of the greens into the water.

When you find an abundant supply of water-cress you can dry and store it for future use as a mild seasoning.

Some people make water-cress tea, either out of the fresh plant or the dried.

Plantain

Plantago major

Plantain is a weed in lawns, fields and waste places but is also an edible spring green.

The plant is not hard to identify. It has a rosette of broad flat leaves which are parallel-veined and facing in all directions. One or more greenish flower spikes looking rather like pipe cleaners come up in the center of the rosette.

The soft leaves in early spring are good in a green salad and are nutritious, containing vitamins A and C.

The leaves quickly become fibrous so even in spring people often prefer cooking the plant. Use only the leaf blades, not the stalks. If you find the leaves too fibrous for a cooked vegetable, you can make a soup

12

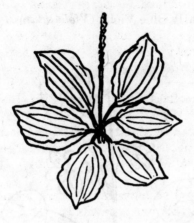

by forcing the cooked leaves through a sieve and adding the resulting puree to a chicken-stock base.

Chopped raw or cooked plantain leaves could be added to omelets, casseroles and stews.

. Some people use the dried leaves for tea.

There are several species of plantain that could be used in the same way as *Plantago major,* which is the common plantain. In Alaska a seaside plantain is canned for winter use.

The seeds of some species are used as a laxative.

A medicinal use for common plantain is to place bruised leaves, which are mildly astringent, over an open wound to prevent infection.

The plant has been known since ancient times and has acquired a good supply of folk lore.

True or not, one belief has it that the root, when "hanged about the necke," would cure "hard swellings about the eares and throte."

The root was also the source of Alexander the Great's greatness. "Held firmly in the left hand," the root was supposed to render the mind "clear and forceful."

We moderns can pooh-pooh the old legends, but we can also say — Well, let's eat the plant and see what the vitamins and minerals will do for us.

Violet

Early Blue Violet *(Viola adunca)*

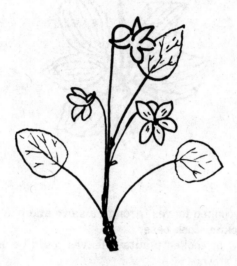

Almost the entire violet plant can be eaten — leaves, flowers, unopened buds and root crown.

There are about 60 species of violets in the United States, some wild, some growing in gardens. You can try any species. Some are better for eating than others.

Some violets have heart-shaped leaves, some have oval, and some lance-shaped. The color of the flowers varies from white to yellow, blue, purple, or combinations of these.

The scientific name for the species is *Viola*, the same as the garden pansy, which was developed from hybrids of European and Asiatic violets.

The violet pictured is the early blue violet, *Viola adunca*. It grows in moist shady soil and is found over most of North America. The blue-violet flower appears May to July.

Viola adunca has been tested for nutritive value and it is extremely rich in vitamins A and C.

Violet leaves added to a salad of head lettuce make up for the vitamins the lettuce doesn't have. The leaves cooked as greens are mild-tasting and very nutritious. If you find the taste so mild that is is flat you could add a portion of dandelion greens.

In southern Unites States there is a violet that is called wild okra because it is used to give soup the same mucilaginous quality okra does.

Violet vinegar can be made by adding blossoms to white wine vinegar.

You can dry the leaves for tea. There is so much vitamin C in the leaves that even dried they are a good source. Sweetening with honey will add flavor. You can also add one or two dried dandelion leaves or a mint leaf.

The sweet blue violet of Europe, immortalized by "My Fair Lady" and its cockney flower vendor, is grown commercially in Europe and the near East, not only for sale as a flower but also to make perfume. In Egypt and Turkey there is a drink called sorbet, which is violet sugar dissolved in water.

In the days when candied flowers were considered a proper sweet, violets were much used. A thick sugar syrup was made and the fresh flowers were dipped in the syrup and then put on a plate to dry.

There is vitamin C in the flowers so the candy-eaters were getting some nutritive value.

Historians say the violet was the favorite flower of both Mohammed and Napoleon.

Asparagus

Asparagus officinalis

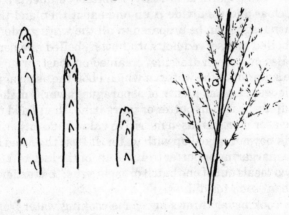

Wild asparagus is exactly the same as garden asparagus. It should be because it is the same plant, *Asparagus officinalis*.

It has been known as a cultivated plant since old Roman days. Emperor Augustus was fond of it and Cato the Roman patriot wrote down directions for growing it. He said to start with the seed of the wild plant, which was found then in parts of Europe, the Caucasian regions and Siberia.

Asparagus is not native to the United States. It was imported from Europe and the birds spread the seeds from the garden to the wild.

It is a perennial, meaning that the roots stay alive and send up new stalks every year. A plant that is called an annual dies completely at the end of the growing season and only seeds remain to sprout and start new growth the next spring.

The part of the asparagus you eat are the new shoots which come up in late spring, around May and June. The shoots look like fat fingers poking through the ground. The shoots grow up and turn into flowering stalks that can be five feet tall. The stalks are branched and covered with a soft green lacy growth much like the new needles on larch trees.

The greenish flowers are inconspicuous but they are followed by berries which turn red and are eaten by birds.

The stalks turn straw-colored and often stay rooted in the ground through winter. The lacy foliage is worn off by the wind and snow but the dry bare stalks are a signpost for spring asparagus hunters.

The wise hunter spots the dry stalks and then keeps the location secret until the succulent shoots come through the ground.

Riverbanks are a favorite spot but you can also find wild asparagus on hillsides, along railroad tracks and along irrigation canals. There is nothing to compare with asparagus picked fresh and rushed home and cooked immediately. Cook it only a minute or two.

Actually raw asparagus is a tasty tidbit. My students often bring a fat shoot to class and we divide it up and eat it then and there.

Wild asparagus can be prepared in all the ways garden asparagus is used — boiled and served hot with butter, boiled and served cold with mayonnaise or French dressing, creamed on toast, or made into soup.

I make soup out of the water in which I boil the asparagus. Since I use very little water it has plenty of asparagus flavor. I make a roux base, which is flour heated in butter or margarine, then I add the asparagus cooking water. For increased nutritive value I add either whole milk or dried milk powder mixed up with water. If I use the dried milk powder I add extra margarine or butter to make up for the lack of fat in the milk.

I get two meals out of one batch of asparagus: the tender tips for lunch and a cream soup for dinner.

A good cook never throws away the cooking water from vegetables. Even potato water can be used in soups. Some people simply drink the vegetable water. It has good amounts of vitamins in it.

Gathering wild asparagus is a test of a person's character. First of all, you have to consider private property. That asparagus, even though wild, might belong to somebody. Second, even if it is on public land, should you feel free to cut all of it.

I tell my students to be happy with a little, to leave some for other searchers, and to leave some to grow up into a flowering stalk to renew the food supply in the root system and to develop seeds for the birds to eat and spread to new places.

Wild food of the asparagus type should be considered a novelty rather than a real source of nourishment. You can enjoy the idea of wild food as much as the eating. You have the fun of going out to hunt, you have the fun of gathering, and you have the fun of sharing the food with your family and friends.

Shepherd's-purse

Capsella bursa-pastoris

Shepherd's-purse is one of the most common weeds in the whole world. It is found on every continent, growing in cities and towns, in the country, in gardens, fields — just about everywhere.

The name comes from the shape of the seed pods. If you look closely you will see that the seed pods are flat and heart-shaped, much like the purse used by old-time European shepherds.

The plant originated in Europe and the name originated there too.

There are actually four or five species all called shepherd's-purse and looking very much alike. *Capsella bursa-pastoris* is the most common one.

It is a small plant, never growing taller than 18 inches. The flowers are so tiny you hardly notice them. They are white and four-petaled.

They turn into the conspicuous triangular seeds everyone recognizes.

The leaves are two shapes. The upper leaves clasp the stem and are more or less arrow-shaped. The basal leaves can be almost entire or cut like those of the dandelion.

The basal leaves are edible when young. The taste is slightly bitter

17

and peppery. Since shepherd's-purse is in the mustard family that is not surprising.

The seeds have been used as meal by the Indians. If you look at the size of the seed pod you can imagine the size of the seeds and you can appreciate the patience of anyone who would gather them for food.

We would probably find the taste a bit strong. Actually the seeds have been used medicinally as a mild tonic.

The roots, which also have a peppery taste, have been used as a substitute for ginger.

The name *Capsella* means little box. *Bursa-pastoris* means shepherd's purse.

Pennycress, or fanweed, is a close relative of shepherd's-purse except that the seed pods are larger and rounder, and the basal leaves are not dandelion-shaped.

Fireweed

Epilobium angustifolium

Fireweed can be useful on a camping trip. It is plentiful and is eaten raw or cooked. Like many green plants, it can supply vitamins A and C.

Spring is the best time to eat the plant since the young shoots are tender and more palatable than the older plant which becomes tough and bitter. However, the difficulty with eating the young shoots is identification when you don't have the flowering stalk to help you. Unless you go on a field trip with an expert you will probably have to identify the plant first during flowering season and then keep an eye on it for the next spring.

A common habitat is burned-over land. As you can guess from the name, fireweed comes after fires. It also follows logging work and road clearings. The seeds have the ability to travel easily on the wind because each seed has its own parachute of long silky hairs. The plant is a perennial. It stays until trees take over and shade it out.

It is a showy plant that can grow eight feet tall, with pink to purple flowers in a long spike. The blooms at the bottom open first, so there are often unopened buds at the top while the bottom flowers have already turned into seed pods.

The blooms are four-petaled, a characteristic of the evening-primrose family where fireweed belongs.

Other names for the plant are willow-herb and willow-weed (because the leaves resemble those of willow) and blooming Sally (reason unknown).

There are over a dozen species of *Epilobium* in the United States. Several have been used as food.

The young leaves, the peeled stems, and the unopened buds can all be put in salad or cooked as a potherb or added to soup and stew.

The older leaves can be used for tea, either alone or in combination with other herbs.

Fireweed is a good bee plant. You have probably eaten fireweed honey without knowing it.

According to one recipe I found, you can make the honey yourself. The recipe calls for boiling sugar and water into a heavy syrup and then steeping flower petals in the syrup.

I'd rather leave the honey-making to the bees but I like the idea of using the flowers in a tea and then sweetening the tea with a touch of honey.

Lamb's Quarter

Chenopodium album

Lamb's quarter is a wild spinach. It is in the same family as cultivated spinach and if we did not have the cultivated spinach as an established vegetable, tender and easy to grow, we might be developing its wild relative.

As it is, lamb's quarter has two reputations: one as a garden weed which has to be pulled out and thrown away, and the other as a green vegetable richer in vitamins A and C than spinach.

Those of us who are herb-eaters (weed-eaters is another term, not quite so flattering) put lamb's quarter close to the top of the list. It is available, easily identified, and it has a mild taste.

The common lamb's quarter is *Chenopodium album.* There are many other *Chenopodiums,* some of which are also used as food.

The name *Chenopodium album* means white goosefoot and refers to the shape of the leaves and their whitish sheen. The plant is often called white goosefoot.

It is also called pigweed because pigs are very fond of it. They are wise because in eating it they are getting a good ration of vitamins and minerals. However, the name pigweed is confusing for human herb-eaters because there are many other plants called pigweed.

This is a good reason for learning scientific names. If a person tells you that he eats pigweed you can say, "Which pigweed? *Chenopodium album?*"

The plant grows in waste places and some not so waste places such as your vegetable garden. It will reach a height of three or four feet in good soil.

For eating purposes you want young plants less than a foot high.

The leaves are dull green and water does not wet them. It runs off or stands in drops.

The plant can be eaten raw in salad or cooked like spinach. I like a touch of vinegar on the cooked greens.

Lamb's quarter is one of the edible wild plants easiest to obtain. I freeze a dozen or more packages every year.

The only drawback is the same one spinach has. Studies show that eating a great deal of spinach interferes with calcium absorption. In other words, the calcium in your milk might not do you much good if eaten along with spinach.

The culprit in the spinach is oxalates. Other cultivated plants that have high amounts of oxalates are rhubarb, Swiss chard and beet tops. Wild plants are the docks, sorrels, purslane, tumbleweed, miner's lettuce and lamb's quarter.

A varied diet would not include any of these plants too often. Therefore, with a little stress on "moderation in all things," we can eat these foods without ill effects.

The tiny seeds of lamb's quarter, which are produced in tremendous amounts, can be gathered and ground into flour.

However, the seeds are so small you would have a hard time grinding them and the resulting flour is dark and "mousey" tasting. In an emergency you could make bread or gruel (a thin porridge) but otherwise you might as well leave the seeds for the birds.

Strawberry blite *(C. capitatum)* is a plant rather similar to lamb's quarter but it has edible fruit, reddish-colored, in addition to edible leaves.

Prickly Lettuce

Lactuca serriola

Don't expect wild lettuce to look like garden lettuce even though both are in the *Lactuca* genus. If you allow garden lettuce to go to seed then it will have a slight resemblance to its wild cousin.

Prickly lettuce *(Lactuca serriola)* is one of the species of wild lettuce and it is edible when very young. The taste will remind you of dandelion and that is not surprising because lettuce is related to dandelion, chicory and salsify. All these plants have milky juice and dandelion-like

flowers. They also tend to be bitter. The name *Lactuca* is from the Latin for milk.

Cultivated lettuce has been perfected to produce plenty of tender leaves and even heads. The wild lettuces go straight to seed as fast as possible. That, after all, is the purpose of plants. They have to produce seeds as fast as possible to insure perpetuation of the species.

Prickly lettuce can be eaten raw in salad or cooked as a potherb but it must be picked when the plant is only a few inches high. The season lasts about a week.

The plant grows in waste places, open fields, and even in cities right along the sidewalks. In fact, it is so common it is a pest.

The flowering stems can be four feet tall, with many small pale yellow flowers. The leaves are like those of a dandelion but have weak spines along the midrib. They are bluish-green in color.

There is a bitter taste to the plant even when young and it persists even if parboiled. People who relish a bitter taste, cook wild lettuce in the Chinese way, which is using only the moisture that adheres to the leaves when washed. This is a good way to cook any vegetable in order to preserve as much of the vitamin and mineral content as possible. Heat a little oil, butter, margarine or bacon fat in a sauce pan, toss in the washed greens and cover. As soon as the vegetable is limp, it is ready to be seasoned and eaten. Of course, if a plant is bitter, this method of cooking will also retain all the bitterness.

Prickly lettuce is native to Europe. It spread to America and now is found almost all over the United States.

It is sometimes called compassplant because its leaves tip and turn until they are vertical instead of horizontal.

In herb medicine, the milky juice has the reputation of being a mild sedative and narcotic.

Blue lettuce *(L. pulchella)* can also be eaten when very young. The flowers are a pretty blue and the leaves are not prickly.

22

Miner's Lettuce

Montia perfoliata

Miner's lettuce is a tiny plant but it can furnish a tasty vitamin-rich salad or potherb. The name tells you it came in handy in the gold-rush days when the Forty-niners needed something to protect them against scurvy. Even as cooked greens, the plant contains vitamin C.

The plant is in the purslane family, the same family as the also edible bitterroot, springbeauty, and purslane.

Miner's lettuce grows as a groundcover, only inches tall. It is an annual, meaning it dies completely at the end of the growing season.

There are two kinds of leaves: basal ones which have long stalks and are spatula-shaped, and a joined pair on the flowering stalk which cup the small pinkish-white flowers.

The succulent plant grows in moist shaded soil in valleys and lower mountains. I have found it under Ponderosa pine.

Other names are Indian lettuce and Spanish lettuce. These names honor the people who helped the miners by introducing them to this native-growing nutritious green plant.

The flowers are edible also so in an emergency you could eat the new young leaves raw or cook the older plant, leaves, flowers and all. The taste is mild.

Curly Dock

Rumex crispus

Curly dock is a spring green that is widely used. It grows all over North America, in the country and in the city. You can find it along sidewalks. As cooked greens, it has an acid taste as if you had already added vinegar.

The plant is in the buckwheat family and has the three-winged seeds characteristic of the family. The seeds become red-brown in winter and are quite conspicuous.

The plant is a perennial with deep roots. The early spring leaves come up in a bunch from the root crown. These leaves can be a foot long and have curly edges, hence the name curly dock. Later the flowering stalk appears, one to three feet tall.

The leaves are edible in spring and then again in fall when a new crop appears. A few people eat them raw in salad but the preferred way is as a potherb. They need little seasoning because they have a lemony taste. They make a good accompaniment with fish.

Most people experience no difficulty in eating dock but it can act as a laxative if eaten in quantity. The root has been used in medicine under the name yellow dock. It acts as a purge and tonic.

There are oxalates in dock, of the same type found in rhubarb and spinach.

There are many species of dock and most of them are edible. Curly dock *(Rumex crispus)*, also called sour dock, is an import from Europe but it has established itself so well it is often a troublesome weed.

The vitamin A content of curly dock is the same as lamb's quarter, and the vitamin C content is higher than either lamb's quarter or dandelion.

The cooked greens lose about half the vitamin C but not much of the vitamin A.

The seeds of many of the docks have been used by the Indians as we use buckwheat today — ground into a meal and then used for bread or mush.

In a time of emergency, winter greens could be obtained from curly dock by the technique of "forcing" which consists of digging the roots in late summer, planting them in a pot in the basement, and watering. The warmth of the basement will cause leaves to sprout.

Sheep Sorrel

Rumex acetosella

Sheep sorrel makes a tasty wild salad. Just pick the soft green leaves and eat. They have a natural tart taste that is refreshing and you do not need salad dressing.

The plant is a weed in fields, along roadsides and in odd corners right in the middle of cities.

A member of the buckwheat family, it can be recognized by the buckwheat-shaped seeds growing along the flowering stalk.

The scientific name, *Rumex acetosella,* tells you that the plant is in the same genus as curly dock. The leaves of curly dock are edible also and they have the same tart taste.

Sheep sorrel is a perennial, growing from four to 15 inches tall. The light green arrow-shaped (halbert-shaped is more accurate) leaves are sometimes only an inch long but in a plant growing in rich soil they can be larger.

The flowers are small and inconspicuous. It is the clusters of seeds, first green then red, that are noticeable.

The sour-tasting leaves have been eaten in many parts of the world. A similar plant, *Rumex acetosa,* is actually cultivated in Europe and Asia and is called garden sorrel. It is a taller plant, up to three feet, and the leaves can be six inches long. The well-known sorrel soup of France is a delicacy.

Since the *Rumex* genus has the same type of oxalates that rhubarb has it is probably best not to eat sheep sorrel in large amounts. Livestock have been poisoned by over-eating of this plant.

However, adding the leaves to salads or flavoring an omelet or soup will not overload your system. Some people sprinkle the chopped leaves on fish, potatoes and rice.

In the wilderness, the leaves add a piquant touch to sandwiches or stews. You can make a lemonade-like drink by simmering the leaves and then drinking the water.

The seeds have been used as food and could be counted on in an emergency.

Rumex acetosella is a European import, now growing throughout North America, with many common names: sour weed for one, also red, cow, mountain, field, horse or sheep sorrel.

Mountain sorrel is generally reserved for a different plant — also edible — *Oxyria digyna.*

Mountain Sorrel

Oxyria digyna

Mountain sorrel is a handy plant to know if you are hiking in mountain country. Nibbling on the tart leaves quenches your thirst and revives your strength.

The plant is in the same family — the buckwheat — as sheep sorrel and curly dock. All these plants have a lemony taste and all are edible. They contain oxalates like spinach and rhubarb so it is recommended not to eat any of them to excess. Oxalates in the form of oxalic acid can be harmful to the kidneys.

26

Mountain sorrel *(Oxyria digyna)* is a clump-style plant, a perennial growing from a fleshy taproot. The leaves are small and round or kidney-shaped. They can be reddish-tinged. The flowering stalk varies in height from a few inches to a foot and a half.

The flowers are hardly noticeable. They turn into reddish seed capsules that are arranged along the flowering stems in the same manner as those of dock or sheep sorrel.

The plant is found in alpine and subalpine regions all over the world. It grows in moist soil.

Alpine sorrel is one of the common names. Others are sour grass and scurvy grass. Mountain sorrel probably compares in vitamin C content to sheep sorrel and the docks so it is a valuable plant and deserves the name scurvy grass.

However, many plants are called scurvy grass so you cannot identify *Oxyria digyna* by that name. The same goes for sour grass.

The plant was widely used, both raw and cooked, by the Indians. One method of preparation was to mix it with other greens, water-cress for instance, and ferment it like **sauerkraut.**

Another method was to boil the sorrel with salmon roe and berries then dry the mixture in the sun. The resulting "cakes" could be stored for winter use, carried along on trips, or used as an article of trade.

Hikers can use the tart leaves raw as a substitute for lettuce or cooked as an addition to trail soups and stews.

The plant grows in Alaska and the Eskimos are fond of it.

Nettle

Urtica dioica

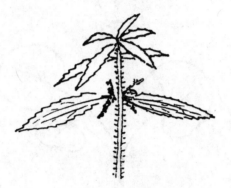

Stinging nettle is known as a pest, but we can also consider it an edible spring green. You will need gloves and a knife to collect it, but after it is cooked the stinging property disappears.

The plant has to be used when young, about six to eight inches tall, as the stalks get very tough. As a matter of fact, you can make a twine out of old dried stalks.

The plant is a perennial, growing two to six feet tall, often in clumps. The flowers are greenish and inconspicuous. The opposite leaves are lance-shaped and toothed. The stems are covered with bristly hairs which contain a substance that burns or stings.

The Latin name for stinging neetle is *Urtica dioica. Urtica* comes from the Latin *uro,* to burn. A word called urtication comes from the ancient practice of doctors lashing patients with nettle branches on the theory of setting up counter-irritation to the original ailment.

There are several varieties of *Urtica dioica,* some with longer thinner leaves, some with shorter blunter leaves. Sometimes the leaves are hairy. The plants grow along streams and in waste places where the ground is moist.

Young nettles are tender and require little cooking. The flavor is delicate and you can serve them as plain cooked greens. Cream of nettle soup would also be good, or a nettle omelet.

If you can dig or pull the young plant, you will find a length of pink underground stem. This is tender and can be boiled along with the tops.

The nutritional value of nettle consists of vitamins A and C, some minerals and an unusually high percentage of protein. One does not usually think of green plants as a source of protein but nettle could be an emergency source. The dried plant is 40 per cent protein.

Nettle has been used for centuries, both for animal feed and for humans. Samuel Pepys mentions being served "Nettle porridge." Thomas Campbell, the British poet, said "In Scotland, I have eaten Nettles, I have slept in Nettle sheets, and I have dined off a Nettle tablecloth..."

He could also have mentioned nettle beer, wine and tea. Nettle tea has a mild flavor. It has been used in Europe as a substitute for coffee and Oriental tea.

One recipe I found for using the nettle plant is not for ordinary menus but it could be used for the survival stewpot. It is a thick soup made of young nettle shoots, ants, and a dozen minnows, heads and all.

Chickweed

Stellaria media

Chickweed is a green plant that can be found almost year round. There often are new plants in late summer and fall. In protected spots they can survive the winter.

The straggly sprawling plant has the scientific name *Stellaria media* and it is important to use that name because chickweed alone could mean several plants: field chickweed, for instance, is in the same family but a different genus — *Cerastium*.

Stellaria media is sometimes called common chickweed in order to differentiate it from the others. It came from Europe and is now widespread in the United States and considered a pest. However, it can also be considered a vitamin-rich green, good raw or cooked.

The weak, delicate stems, four to 16 inches long, grow prostrate on the ground. The small leaves are opposite on the stem. The flowers are white, five-petaled and tiny.

Chickweed grows in both city and country: in gardens, lawns, alleys and cultivated fields. It likes moist soil and partial shade.

As a potherb, boil the plant like spinach and serve with butter or margarine. Some people season with vinegar but I find the taste good alone.

In a tossed salad the small green leaves add color, taste and vitamins.

The leaves can be dried and used as a tea. Tea made from the fresh plant would be a richer source of vitamin C.

The tiny seeds which form in a podlike capsule can be collected and used as food for birds.

Of course if the plant is a pest in your garden, it is best not to allow the seedpods to form. They might burst and scatter their seeds before you collected them for the birds and then next year you would have an even bigger crop of common chickweed. It is better to eat the plant as fast as it comes up.

The family of the chickweeds is *Caryophyllaceae* which is the pink family. It is interesting to note that the color pink came from the flowers of this family, many of which are pink or rose-colored, but the original meaning of the word had nothing to do with color. The base of the word pink is pinken which in Old English means to scallop or pink out and it refers to the cleft edges of the flower petals.

Amaranth

Amaranthus retroflexus

Amaranth, also called green amaranth or rough pigweed, is an edible green that is easy to find. It grows even in city streets.

You really have to use the scientific name, *Amaranthus retroflexus*, when referring to this plant because there are many plants called pigweed. If a plant grew around farmyards and the pigs ate it, the name pigweed was attached.

Amaranth is sometimes called wild beet or redroot because the root is red and looks rather like an undeveloped beet.

The new leaves of amaranth are just as edible as beet greens. Maybe you don't eat beet greens. You should because they are loaded with vitamin A and iron. Amaranth greens have the same content of vitamin A and iron and are also rich in vitamin C.

The taste of amaranth greens is mild. Therefore, season with butter and vinegar or mix the amaranth greens with a stronger-flavored green such as dandelion or mustard.

You must gather the amaranth when the plant is only inches high. If

30

you are a newcomer to edible wild foods, you may not be able to identify the plant until the flowering stalk appears and then it will be too late for tender greens. However, you can spot the gathering place and be ready for next year.

Amaranth is an annual, growing one to five feet tall. The leaves are ovate, and the flower stalk is like a pale green cockscomb. The red cockscomb we plant in our garden is in the same family — the amaranth.

The name *Amaranthus* means "unfading" and it refers to the unfading color of the flower stalk, which is actually made up of stiff sepal scales, not petals.

Amaranth seeds are small and shiny black. The Indians parched them and ate them whole or ground them into a meal. "Pinole" is a name attached to edible seeds of this kind.

We would find the meal blackish in color and weedy in taste.

The Indians used the greens as a potherb. Some tribes actually encouraged the plant to grow near their camps.

The Indians also used the greens and seeds of a prostrate amaranth — *A. graecizans*.

Purslane

Portulaca oleracea

Purslane is an edible green that is very easy to find because it is a weed that grows unwanted in our gardens. It even grows in window

31

boxes.

It is sometimes called low pigweed and certainly pigs will eat it — with relish — as will cattle.

It is also called pusley and common purtulaca. The latter name will give you a hint as to what family purslane is in — the portulaca family, the same as bitterroot, springbeauty and the garden portulaca.

The scientific name is *Portulaca oleracea*. The plant grows close to the ground, sprawling like a ground cover. The leaves and stems are fleshy. The flowers are hardly noticeable but the many tiny seeds fall from a mature plant like a shower.

Purslane is actually cultivated in some countries and sold in the market. It can be eaten raw or cooked.

The taste is mild and pleasant, with a slightly acid touch. Thoreau wrote: "I have made a satisfactory dinner on several accounts, simply off a dish of Purslane which I gathered in my cornfield, boiled and salted."

The stems and leaves are succulent and give body to casseroles. One recipe suggests a dish of purslane, eggs and bread crumbs.

Adding purslane to soup thickens it in the way okra does. Some people object to this mucilaginous quality, calling it a "fatty" feel.

Purslane as a health food is very high in iron, besides containing a goodly quantity of vitamins A and C. The 16th century herbalist, John Gerard, wrote: "It cools the blood and causes appetite."

In the southwest purslane grows among the sagebrush and cattle get fat on it.

The tiny seeds can be gathered and ground into a meal or flour. The color is blackish and the taste "buckwheaty" but a portion in hot cakes makes a novel touch.

If your garden this summer is heavily invaded by purslane, you can freeze it like spinach and store it for winter. It will save you buying greens and you will clear your garden of a "weed" at the same time.

I myself look forward to a little purslane among my tomato plants and I only pinch off the tips and let the plant keep on going.

Bracken

Pteridium aquilinum

Bracken is a coarse fern having tall leafy fronds that die in autumn. Also called brake, it grows in patches in open spaces.

The young coiled shoots, called fiddleheads, are edible but they must be prepared properly. The woolly cover must be rubbed off as it has toxic qualities. The shoots are bitter and when they are being boiled, the water may have to be changed several times. Mature fronds have more of the poison.

The roots are plump rhizomes and were used by Indians for food but the taste would not be appealing to us. Captain Meriwether Lewis described the taste as disagreeably pungent.

Bracken is *Pteridium aquilinum* and it grows all over the world. There are twelve varieties, all called bracken or brake or brake-fern.

In times of famine, bread could be made from the roots of certain varieties but it would be rather bitter.

The fronds do not grow in clusters like most ferns. They grow singly from the creeping rootstocks. They can grow as tall as six or eight feet but the average height is three feet.

The new fiddlehead shoots have three prongs.

The variety of bracken found in the Rockies is *Pteridium aquilinum pubescens*. The frond has a triangular shape.

In autumn the fronds change to a rusty color. The dead fronds are cover for wildlife. In some countries they are used for animal fodder and for thatching roofs.

To indicate the care that must be taken when trying to use bracken as food, keep in mind that a strong tea made of the plant has been used to get rid of intestinal worms.

Even the young shoots should not be used over a prolonged period of time, as the plant destroys thiamine (vitamin B$_1$) in the body.

This is one reason more studies have to be made before widespread preservation of wild plants can be recommended. The Indians used most plants only during a short season. If we start canning these plants, hoping to eat them regularly, we are changing the use pattern and we should go slowly.

Few experiments on long-term use of wild plants have been made.

Cow-parsnip

Heracleum lanatum

Cow-parsnip was the wild rhubarb of the Indians. In early spring they looked forward to gathering a mess of the new tender shoots and boiling them or roasting them over coals.

The early "voyageurs" were so happy to have this green to boil along with their pemmican they called it a "grateful" vegetable.

Cow-parsnip is easy to spot. It is a coarse plant growing three to eight feet tall with large toothed leaves and a flat-topped umbel of white flowers. Both leaves and flowerhead are sometimes a foot across.

The flower structure reminds you of an over-sized Queen Anne's lace, and that is suitable because both are in the parsley family.

Cow-parsnip is eaten by cows, as the name suggests, and also by sheep, bears, elk and marmots. Other common names of the plant are cow-cabbage, Hercules-parsnip and masterwort.

The scientific name, *Heracleum lanatum*, refers to the larger-than-life hero Hercules and to the woolly aspect of the leaves and stem.

The roots were cooked and eaten by Indians but the taste would not appeal to us.

The stems can be eaten but they must be peeled because the juice and hairs of the rind may cause blisters.

Actually not many people use cow-parsnip as a food today. The taste to modern appetites is rank and weedy even if parboiled. Also there is danger in the parsley family. There are two very poisonous members in the family — water-hemlock and poison-hemlock. When the plants are fully grown and in bloom identification is not so difficult but if you were hiking in early spring and the plants were only six inches tall you might run into trouble. It is best to leave the cow-parsnip to the cows.

The term "sacred rhubarb" is sometimes connected with this plant because it was used in the Blackfeet Indian Sun Dance ceremony.

The plant grows in damp soil and can be seen along stream banks and in open woods up to 8,500 feet altitude. The flowering season is May to July.

Stonecrop

Yellow Stonecrop *(Sedum stenopetalum)*

The stonecrops, also called sedums, are fleshy succulents usually growing in rocky gravelly soil. Several species are edible, including yellow stonecrop *(Sedum stenopetalum),* which is quite common and grows at all altitudes from valleys to above timberline.

The stonecrops are able to grow in arid soil because they retain large amounts of moisture in their thick leaves.

The genus name *Sedum* comes from the Latin to sit and refers to the way the plants affix themselves to rocks and gravel beds.

The narrow cylindrical leaves of yellow stonecrop are greenish-brown or reddish-brown and form rosettes. The flowering stalk, three to eight inches tall, comes up in the center and has yellow star-like flowers.

Yellow stonecrop can be eaten raw or cooked. The young leaves and shoots are best. Older ones tend to become tough and bitter. It is advised to eat only a small amount as stonecrop does not agree with everyone.

A pink-flowered species, *S. rhodanthum,* also edible, grows taller than yellow stonecrop and has the leaves along the flower stalk instead of in rosettes. Common names for this species are queen's crown or rose crown.

A rose-colored species that grows in the Arctic is much used by the Eskimos. They eat it fresh, pickled or preserved in oil. The common name is roseroot.

The yellow-flowered garden sedum called mossy stonecrop or wallpepper *(S. acre)* has tiny fat leaves that taste peppery and have been used as an addition to cole slaw.

Marsh-marigold

Caltha palustris   Caltha leptosepala

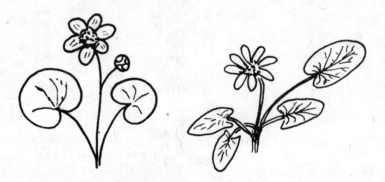

There is an eastern marsh-marigold and a western one. Both species grow in wet places and have glossy leaves and flowers like large buttercups.

The eastern marsh-marigold has bright yellow flowers and it is the species generally called cowslip. However, cowslip is really a confusing name because many flowers are called that. What Shakespeare and other British writers referred to as cowslip is a primula. Marsh-marigold is probably the best name, unless you want to use the botanical name.

Back in the Middle Ages in Europe the yellow-flowered *Caltha* was called Mary-buds. This could be the origin of the name marigold. Our garden marigolds are not *Caltha*. They are in the daisy family. The *Caltha* genus is in the buttercup family.

The leaves of the eastern marsh-marigold *(Caltha palustris)* were cooked and eaten by both Indians and settlers. This is the same species found in the Arctic and used by the Alaskans today. They boil both the green plant and the roots.

The plant is bitter. Most people boil it in two waters to remove some of the strong taste.

The western white marsh-marigold *(Caltha leptosepala)* is even bitterer than *C. palustris*. It has not been used to the extent that *C. palustris* has.

Both the eastern and western species are mentioned as possibly toxic. There is a poisonous glucoside in the *Caltha* genus that has killed cattle. Elk apparently are not affected by the glucoside. They eat the plant without danger. In fact, white marsh-marigold is called elk marsh-marigold and elkslip.

The glucoside is volatile and is removed by heat so cooking the plant renders it safe. Also the young plant has little of the poisonous principle. Some people feel confident enough to use the young leaves as a salad.

The unopened buds of the eastern species have been pickled as a substitute for capers.

Evening-primrose

Common Evening-primrose

Oenothera biennis

Evening-primrose opens its flowers in the evening. The fragile blossoms last only until the hot sun of the next day.

In this short span a night-flying insect — generally a moth — pollinates the flower.

Each plant has many buds and only one opens per day so the over-all blooming period of a group of plants is quite long. The height of the season is July and August.

Oenothera biennis is the common field and roadside evening-primrose. In some places it is so common it is considered a weed.

The plant grows from one to four feet tall and has a hairy stem and leaves. The four yellow petals form a flower that is rather square in shape. The seeds are narrow pods about an inch long.

Several species of evening primrose are edible. The Indians dried the roots for winter use. They also used the seedpods and the ripe seeds.

The early colonists used the young shoots of *Oenothera biennis* as a potherb. In some places they cultivated the plant so they would have a steady supply of the roots to use like parsnips. You can find oldtime recipes saying to cut up the evening-primrose roots and put them in gumbo soup.

We who have many vegetables to choose from would find the *Oenothera* genus too bitter for our taste.

In Europe the edible species of evening-primrose is called wild beet and German rampion.

Oenothera means wine-scented in Greek. Some of the evening-primroses have a delicious fragrance.

Several species are garden plants. Some are annuals, some are biennials and some are perennial. The flowers of some of the yellow species fade to red when they age, and some of the white-flowered species fade to pink.

In the wild the common evening-primrose can give you a pleasant surprise on a camping trip. You think you are setting up your tent in a rather bare field. Then the sun goes down and all of a sudden it's like pop goes the evening-primrose — and you are camped in a field of yellow blossoms.

Yellow Wood-sorrel

Oxalis stricta

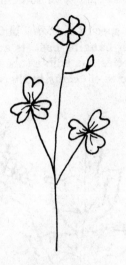

Yellow wood-sorrel is a flower (also a weed) that grows in gardens and sometimes in woods or along roadsides.

It is a small plant with three-parted leaves like clover, and upright stems. There are usually two or three yellow five-petaled flowers — sometimes more, as many as seven. Both flowers and leaves close at night.

The leaves have an acid taste and some people eat them.

The wood-sorrel generally mentioned in edible-plant information is the common one of eastern U.S. — originally from Europe — *Oxalis acetosella*. It is used in salads and sandwiches. It has white flowers with rose-colored veins.

There is much discussion about *Oxalis acetosella* and the Irish shamrock. Was the original Irish shamrock *Oxalis acetosella*? Or was it a clover — *trifolium repens,* or a medick — *Medicago lupulina?* The leaves of all three plants are similar, and it is the leaves that we think of as the shamrock.

The common *Oxalis* of the Rockies is the yellow-flowered *O. stricta.* The similar *O. corniculata* is found here too. It also has yellow flowers but it grows in a creeping manner. It is called creeping yellow wood-sorrel. The leaves can be green or purple.

Violet wood-sorrel grows on the prairie east of the Rockies. The Indians who ate the leaves of that species gave it a name meaning "sour-like-salt."

All the *Oxalis* species contain some oxalic salts so it is best we eat the plants sparingly.

The word *Oxalis* is from the Greek for sour. Most of the species have a sour taste.

There are many garden species of *Oxalis* but most of them are quite delicate. They are good for hanging baskets and pot plants.

One of the Mexican species has edible tubers.

There are over 800 species of *Oxalis* in the world.

Mustard

Black Mustard *(Brassica nigra)*

Mustard is a yellow condiment commonly used on hot dogs but it is also a plant of the same family as cabbage, cauliflower, turnip and broccoli.

This family is not native to the U.S.A. The plants were brought from Europe or Asia. The mustard plants escaped from cultivation and are now found in the wild. There are four or five wild mustards.

Black mustard, *Brassica nigra,* is found around agricultural fields and can become a pest. It grows about six feet tall, with rough hairy leaves and clusters of yellow flowers.

The flowers, like all members of both the mustard genus and the mustard family, have four petals.

The leaves are lobed and toothed. They are edible. You can buy mustard greens in the market, generally of the species *Brassica juncea,* which also grows as a wild plant and is called by many names: brown mustard, leaf mustard, Chinese mustard, Indian mustard (the Indian refers to the Asiatic origin of the plant).

Mustard greens have a strong taste and have to be cooked longer than spinach.

The condiment sold under the name mustard is a paste made of ground mustard seeds, generally *Brassica nigra,* or a mixture of *nigra, hirta* (white mustard), and *juncea,* plus flour, salt, vinegar and turmeric.

The seeds are also sold whole or ground into a powder. As a condiment, mustard is good for digestion.

The use of mustard as a plaster for chest colds is based on the idea that it irritates the skin and stimulates the flow of blood, thus making a person feel "warm."

Mustard plants can be poisonous to livestock. The seeds seem to be the part that is toxic.

When used as greens for the table, the young basal leaves are preferred. They grow large, four to six inches long, and are lyre-shaped.

Charlock is a wild mustard similar to black mustard. Rape is a cultivated mustard, grown for its oil which is used commercially. The seeds of the mustard plants are in pods.

Milkweed

Showy Milkweed *(Asclepias speciosa)*

Milkweed is considered both an edible plant and a poisonous plant. It is a roadside wildflower more common in eastern U.S.A. but there are several species in the west.

Showy milkweed, also called pink milkweed, is a common species. It grows to five feet tall and has large coarse fleshy leaves growing opposite on the stem. The flowers are pinkish or purplish and grow in clusters. The plant grows in open spaces, often in patches. It flowers in early summer.

41

Several species of milkweed, including showy milkweed, *Asclepias speciosa,* can be eaten but care must be taken. In order to have tender shoots the spring growth must be gathered when it is only six or eight inches tall. At this stage it is not easy to identify plants. You would not want to gather the poisonous false hellebore by mistake. The slightly poisonous dogbane can also be confused with milkweed.

It is best to leave milkweed alone unless you have visted the gathering spot the summer and fall before and have identified the plant in its flower and fruit stages.

All milkweeds can be poisonous under certain conditions. For instance, even *A. speciosa* can do damage to livestock if it is eaten in quantity. And one species, *A. subverticillata,* is called poison milkweed.

For people who know enough about wild foods to recognize which milkweed to eat, the young shoots can be a substitute for asparagus. The cooking water has to be changed several times to remove the bitter taste.

The new flower buds can be boiled and eaten and later in the season the young seed pods can be eaten.

The flowers have sugar in them and could be boiled down to make a sweet syrup.

As you would guess from the name, milkweed has a milky juice. This juice, called latex, dries into a rubberlike gum. Some Indian tribes used the dried sap as chewing gum. It has also been used as an antiseptic.

The leaves and roots of many milkweed species have been used as medicine by both Indians and whites.

The medicinal quality of the *Asclepias* genus has been recognized for centuries. The scientific name comes from the Greek god of medicine, *Asklepios*.

The conspicuous seed pods of the milkweeds are filled with silky floss which has been used in many ways. You can stuff a pillow or life jacket; you can pad furniture or insulate walls.

The mature dried plant contains fibers that have been used to make cord.

Butterflyweed is a milkweed, *A. tuberosa*.

Cheeseweed

Malva neglecta

Cheeseweed is also called cheeses because the fruits (the seed containers) are flat and round like a wheel of cheese.

The plant is low-growing and creeping, with prostrate stems about a foot long. You find it growing in barnyards and waste places, along roadsides and sometimes in gardens.

The leaves are roundish, with five to seven lobes. The shape reminds you of a leaf from the greenhouse geranium. The small flowers have notched petals and are white or pale lavender.

The young shoots can be eaten raw or cooked. The tiny fruits can be used raw in salads, cooked as a vegetable, or added to soup. They have a pleasant taste. Some people add them to mixed pickles.

Herb tea can be made from the young leaves.

Soup made from the green plant has a mucilaginous quality, like that

43

imparted by adding okra. This is not surprising because okra is in the same family — the *Malvaceae* or mallow.

There are several mallows that are edible. The name cheeseweed is usually given to *Malva neglecta* but *M. parviflora* can also be called cheeseweed. *M. rotundifolia* is another name for *M. neglecta*.

The name *Malva* is from the Greek for emollient which refers to the mucilaginous juice of some species.

One member of the mallow family has acquired the fame of having a candy named after it. This is the marsh-mallow, which is a plant in the same genus as the garden hollyhock — *Althaea*. The soft glue-like substance in the marsh-mallow roots was used to make the original marshmallow candy. Today we use albumin, gelatin and corn syrup.

The emollient quality was useful in medicine also. A person can swallow a bitter tonic more easily if it has a soft slippery feel.

Cheeseweed came from Europe but it is now so well established in North America it is often considered a pest.

It has a long flowering and fruiting season. You can often find flowers, green fruit and dried fruit on the same plant — starting in June and lasting into late fall.

Mint

Field Mint *(Mentha arvensis)*

Field mint is the most common wild mint. It has square stems and opposite leaves like all members of the mint family. It grows one to three feet high and has clusters of lavender, pink or white flowers in the axils of the leaves.

There are about 25 species of mint. Some are grown commercially for the volatile oil which is contained in the plant and is used to flavor food, medicines, tooth paste and liqueurs.

Field mint, *Mentha arvensis,* can be used exactly like the commercially grown mints. You can pick the leaves and extract the aromatic oil.

The plant grows in wet meadows and around streams. It flowers in midsummer.

Field mint is native to the United States as well as to Eurasia. Two less common mints — peppermint *(M. piperita)* and spearmint *(M. spicata)* are European species introduced into the U.S. All three are found in the wild and can be used to flavor foods and beverages.

You can shred fresh mint leaves in a salad or serve as garnish with lamb or venison. You can make mint jelly or mint tea.

A rather exotic recipe, recommended by a Canadian source, is "boiled snake in mint sauce."

Since the oil that produces the characteristic mint smell is very volatile, it is best when drying leaves for tea to dry them out of the sun and then store in a tightly closed container.

When mint is grown commercially for the oil — Oregon has a $9 million industry — the plant is partially dried, shredded, and then the oil is forced out by steam.

Menthol is one of the products obtained commercially from oil of mint.

The mint of the Bible, the "bitter herb" which accompanied the passover lamb, is believed to be *Mentha longifolia.*

If you have a choice, pick spearmint or peppermint as they are preferred over field mint. Peppermint makes the best herb tea and it also serves as a good addition to less flavorful herb teas — clover, for instance.

Mint is easily grown in the garden.

Clover

Red Clover *(Trifolium pratense)*

Clover is an agricultural crop, a wildflower, and also an edible plant.

There are conflicting theories on how edible clover is. Until more experiments on the digestibility are made we should probably limit our use to herb tea and a few leaves or blossoms added to soup and stews.

There is a high protein content in clover and perhaps in the future scientists will find ways to use it directly for human consumption. Now livestock eats the clover and then we eat the livestock.

There are many clovers, some annual, some perennial. Some grow

only a few inches tall, some two feet.

The flowers are in heads or spikes, and the color varies from pink to purple to yellow and white. The fragrant blossoms are almost synonymous with bees. Clover, bees and honey are closely connected. Bees are necessary for clover to reproduce and in return bees collect the nectar and make large quantities of excellent honey.

There are about 75 species of clover in the U.S., some native, some imported.

Red clover *(Trifolium pratense)* is an import. It has purple-red flowers and the three leaflets which are characteristic of the clover genus. *Trifolium* means three-leaved.

Red clover and two other imports, white clover *(T. repens)* and Alsike clover *(T. hybridum),* are the three main cultivated species.

Clover is grown for its value as animal feed but it is also important for its nitrogen-fixing quality. Clover, like many other members of the pea family, can take nitrogen from the air and change it into compounds that enrich the soil.

The production of honey is a third benefit.

Many of the clovers are edible. The Indians used the entire plant. They took the precaution of dipping it in salt water if they were going to eat it raw.

We can follow that same principle or we can use the leaves only in cooked dishes, and then in limited amounts.

Bloating occurs in livestock from over-eating and it might occur in humans.

Clover blossoms have many uses. They have been used in famine times as a source of bread. Both the seeds and dried blossoms were used.

We can dry the blossoms for tea. If we follow the example of the Indians, we will steam the blossoms before drying them.

A mint leaf can be added to the tea for a zestier flavor. If you sweeten with honey instead of sugar, you will also enhance the flavor.

An exotic dessert is clover blossom fritters. Use freshly picked blossoms and dip them into a sweetened batter and fry.

The blossoms can be added to salads or nibbled on during a hike. They are sweet, which is natural because they contain the nectar the bees extract to make honey.

The blossoms are sometimes included in homemade cough syrup recipes.

Red clover is the state flower of Vermont.

Sweet-clover

Yellow Sweet-clover *(Melilotus officinalis)*

Sweet-clover is like clover and alfalfa in that it can be eaten but with reservations.

Yellow sweet-clover is a much-branched, bright green plant with many spikes of small pea-like yellow flowers. It is not a true clover but it has the characteristic three leaflets.

The plant can grow five feet tall but along roadsides it sometimes looks like a ground cover. This is because it has been mowed and the cut-off stalk sends out new branches which bloom close to the ground.

Yellow sweet-clover is *Melilotus officinalis*. White sweet-clover, which looks exactly like the yellow except it has white flowers, is *Melilotus alba*. Both species are sometimes called melilot and also honey-clover. The sweet-scented flowers are good "bee pasture." They are also good forage for livestock.

They are not native. They were imported from Europe for cultivation and they escaped to fields and roadsides. You can even find them in city streets. Flowering season is summer into fall.

Some of the European species of *Melilotus* are used to flavor cheese,

47

especially the Swiss sapsago and Gruyere.

You can make a health tea or tisane from the blossoms. Some people add dried mint or dandelion leaves for a peppier flavor.

The pea-like seeds can be used in stews and soups. Dried leaves can also be used in soup. The leaves should be gathered before the blossoms appear.

M. alba was used in olden times in Europe to give a sweet odor to snuff and smoking tobacco and also to put in sachets among clothes to both give a pleasant odor and to keep moths away.

In more modern days the plant has been used in medicine as a source of an anticoagulant, dicoumarin.

This chemical is also associated with livestock poisoning since it develops in spoiled sweet-clover hay.

Alfalfa

Medicago sativa

Alfalfa is a green plant rich in protein. Today it is used as animal food, but in the future, with new methods of extracting plant protein, we may be eating foods enriched with alfalfa just as we now enrich home-baked bread and cookies with soybean flour.

People already eat alfalfa sprouts and use the leaves for herb tea, and you can buy alfalfa tablets in stores, but much more work needs to be done in laboratories before we know whether we can eat alfalfa leaves and derive much benefit.

Many plants have high nutritive value but they are not readily digested by humans, and therefore the nutrients are not assimilated into the body.

Scientists are experimenting with methods of extracting the juice from alfalfa and coagulating the protein in the juice. A curd results which is about 40 per cent protein. This curd can be dried into a powder and added to bread, crackers, hot dogs, or other food products.

Alfalfa originated in the area once known as Persia and was brought to Greece by the invading Medes, hence the scientific name, *Medicago*.

Alfalfa is in the legume family and has the three leaflets of the clovers. The bluish-purple flowers are pea-like and grow in short tight spikes. The plant is perennial, deep-rooted, often bushy, growing one to two and a half feet high.

The seed pod is like a pea pod but twisted into a spiral. When the dried pods open, they spit the seeds far away.

Alfalfa is one of the most valuable hay plants of the United States, earning the name "queen of forages," It can also be plowed under for green manure, adding valuable nitrogen to the soil.

It is an important bee plant. You often see bee boxes around alfalfa fields.

Other common names for the plant are purple medic, trefoil and lucerne.

Besides protein, alfalfa is also rich in vitamins and minerals.

Probably the best use we can make of this plant today is to put sprouted seeds in salads, soups and casseroles. In the future we might be doing more.

Tumbleweed

Salsola kali

Not many people would think of tumbleweed as an edible plant but the new young shoots, when only a few inches tall, can be boiled like spinach. They have a mild taste.

There are other plants called tumbleweed but the common one is *Salsola kali*, also called Russian thistle and wind witch.

The scientific name *Salsola* comes from *salsus*, Latin for salt, and refers to both the habitat of the plant, which is the dry, often alkaline regions, and to the salty taste of the stem and leaves.

Tumbleweed is a much-branched herb that starts out with fleshy succulent leaves then develops stiff, awl-shaped, spine-pointed leaves. As the plant matures, it hardens and bends inward into a dome shape.

In late fall it breaks off at the ground or is uprooted and then is blown about by the wind, becoming a "tumblin' tumbleweed." The hardened spines catch on fences and bushes.

49

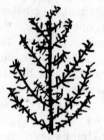

The plant is an annual. The stems are reddish or purplish and grow to three feet tall.

The young plants can be mowed and used as an emergency hay crop.

The flowers are not very noticeable. The seeds have papery wings and are edible. In an emergency, they could be collected and ground into a meal.

The plant, classified in the goosefoot famly, came from Eurasia and is now considered a pest in the United States.

It is found along roadsides, on dry plains and in waste places.

Roots are for
Main Dishes
and
Sometimes a
Beverage

Roots can help you survive if you are lost in the wilderness. Truman Everts, one of the explorers of Yellowstone National Park, lived for a month on the roots of the elk thistle. His horse threw him and he broke his glasses. By luck he was near a patch of elk thistle and in desperation he dug up some of the roots. They nourished him until he was rescued.

Roots contain more nourishment than greens. That is why we include potatoes in our meals. Potatoes are underground tubers attached to the roots. Other forms of root structures are bulbs such as onions, sego lily and camas; corms such as dogtooth violet and springbeauty; rhizomes such as cattail; and fleshy taproots such as salsify and burdock.

The advantages of roots when looking for food in the wild is that, besides containing high calorie value, they are available year round. They can also be kept for a considerable length of time without spoiling.

There are also disadvantages. One, you have to be very careful in identification. The Indians dug many roots after the flowering season was finished. This is dangerous unless you are an expert. Many edible roots look exactly like certain poisonous ones. It is best to use only roots attached to the flowering stalk. Even then examine each root one by one. There is a case where a group of young people were digging cattail rhizomes and a root of the poisonous water-hemlock was lodged among the cattail roots. The results could have been disastrous.

Another disadvantage is that if you dig up the roots of wild plants, you destroy the plant. The bitterroot which is Montana's state flower would become extinct very quickly if we went out and dug up the remaining roots.

The grizzly bear digs up dogtooth violet, springbeauty, and other bulbs, and eats them. He destroys the plants when he does that, but we have to acknowledge that he is in his rights. Foraging is a necessity for

51

the wild animals. It is only a hobby with us unless we are lost in the wilderness like Truman Everts.

We should learn which roots are edible but we should use that knowledge with discretion.

Cattail

Typha latifolia

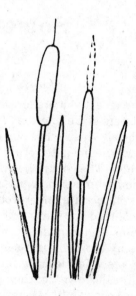

The cattail must be put at the top of the list of edible wild plants. It fulfills all the criteria for what an edible wild plant should be.

Number one, anyone can recognize the cattail. It is a very distinctive plant. Two, there is no poisonous plant that looks anything like it. Three, the cattail has edible parts at all times of the year. Four, it is easily found. Five, it is plentiful and in no danger of extinction. Six, it can do you no harm even if eaten in quantity. Seven, it is easy to prepare. Eight, it tastes good.

There are two species of cattail: one with narrow leaves, *Typha angustifolia,* and one with wide leaves, *Typha latifolia*. Both are edible but *Typha latifolia,* the common cattail, is the one generally used. It grows in marshes all over the world. It has long flat straplike leaves and one flowering stem, three to eight feet tall, topped by a flower spike that is green when new and dark brown when old.

The lower part of the spike is the cluster of female flowers which turns into the "cat tail." Just above is the male part with the pollen. Once the male flowers shed their pollen, they blow away and leave a bare stem on top of the cattail.

The brown cattails stay on the plant until winter and sometimes right through winter.

One of the pieces of advice given to hikers and campers is "If you are lost, head for a cattail marsh." There is no need to go hungry if you can find cattails. Even in fall and winter you can find sustenance. Marshes are often the last environment to freeze in winter and the first to thaw in spring.

The rootstocks of the cattail are edible year round. They are rope-like rhizomes found just below the surface of the ground. They are fibrous but in between the fiber is a quantity of white starch. In an emergency, you could chew on the raw root and get nourishment. Or you could roast it near a fire and then chew on it.

People who have time and want to experiment make flour out of the roots. This is done in several ways. You start by washing and peeling the freshly dug roots then crushing them.

One way to proceed now is to make believe you are washing clothes. Take a bucket of water, immerse the crushed roots and rub them between the hands until the starch comes out and settles to the bottom of the pail. This method is quite hard on the hands.

Method two is to grind the roots in a meat grinder then proceed as in method one.

Method three is to dry the peeled rootstocks then pound them up and shift out the flour.

Method four is to boil the crushed roots then either settle out the starch in water or dry the mass and sift it out.

Using the wet flour right away saves you the work and the heat used to dry it. In order to make bread, you have to moisten the flour anyway.

Some people make camp bread out of pure cattail flour but most people add it to a regular wheat flour recipe. Of course in an emergency, you would simply wrap the cattail dough around a stick and put it next to the fire. If you had a piece of tin can, you would lay the dough on that.

Cattail flour has starch, fat and protein, in rather the same proportion as flour made from grains.

When you dig up the cattail roots in fall or winter, you will notice on the new rootstocks little buds which will be the next year's plant. These buds are good raw or cooked.

Starting in spring, the first edible part is the new shoot that comes up from the root buds. It is easy to gather — just yank it up when it is about a foot or two tall. Peel off the outer green leaves and you will have a central core that is about six inches long and white like the inside of a celery stalk. This is good raw or cooked. It was such a favorite food in the Don area of Russia that it has been called Cossack asparagus ever since. It can be cooked like asparagus and served in the same way.

Around July, depending on elevation, you will see the young flower stalks with the green spikes of unopened flowers on top. This is the part called "corn on the cob." Both the male and female spikes can be cooked like corn on the cob and nibbled until you have eaten off all the green buds and are left with a central stalk about the thickness of a pipe cleaner. The green unopened flowers can also be scraped off the core and used in casserole dishes.

July is also the time for collecting the pollen from the male flower spike. Some people collect the entire flowers, complete with pollen. They use the flowers mixed with wheat flour in pancakes, biscuits or muffins. They dry the excess supply in a slow oven to save for future use.

If you want pure pollen, you can walk through a cattail marsh with a plastic sack and shake the flower spikes over the open sack. You will be surprised how much pollen there is on one spike. The pollen can be used fresh or dried. It has the texture of talcum powder and gives a lovely golden yellow color to pancakes and muffins. I add only a tablespoonful or two. Some people add more. Pollen has nutritive value besides adding an interesting flavor.

There are uses for cattail besides food. The seed fluff has been used for insulation and to help a young camper light his fire.

The leaves can be woven into baskets or mats.

Wild animals and birds make wide use of the cattail. Birds use it for cover and as nesting habitat. Red-winged blackbirds in a cattail marsh are a scene we all enjoy.

Muskrats and geese feed on several parts of the plant.

Bulrush

Hardstem Bulrush *(Scirpus acutus)*

If you pull a bulrush and peel the base, you have a tender white heart about three inches long which you can eat raw or cooked. It is crisp, slightly sweet and mild enough so you can eat all you want. Many edible wild foods have a rather "strong" taste and you have to eat them in moderation.

You can also use the new young shoots of bulrush and the rootstocks, either raw or cooked.

The bulrush is a water plant. It grows in marshes and at the edges of

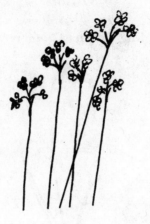

ponds and reservoirs.

There are many species of bulrush. *Scirpus acutus* is hardstem bulrush and grows from 3 to 10 feet tall.

It is also called roundstem bulrush because it has a round stem, dark green in color, without leaves. At the top of the stem are clusters of brown bristly flower spikes.

Some bulrushes have soft, weak stems. Hardstem bulrush has strong stems which dry out but do not decay easily. For this reason, they were used by the Indians for weaving mats.

Throughout history, humans have used the rootstocks for food — raw, cooked or pounded into flour.

The northwest Indians made a sweet syrup by boiling the rootstocks, but it takes up to 15 hours of cooking.

The seeds can be ground into a meal, and the pollen can be used like cattail pollen.

Bulrush is in the *Cyperaceae* family which is the family of the sedges and of papyrus.

Egyptian papyrus is the bulrush of the Bible, associated with the hiding of Moses.

The word tule is also connected with bulrush, but if someone says to you, "I live out in the tules," he usually means simply out in the country, not necessarily in a bulrush marsh.

Onion

Nodding Onion *(Allium cernuum)*

If we did not have the large cultivated onion, we might have to turn to the small wild onion as Lewis and Clark did. On their return trip up the Columbia, before the salmon came, they were living almost entirely on roots. They found the wild onion a welcome addition, both as food value and as an aid to digestion.

In some places wild onion grows so close together it forms a turf.

The cultivated onion is derived from various species of the original wild onion. There are about 300 species of *Allium* in the world. Some are onions, some are chives, some are garlic. There are also leeks and shallots.

A common wild onion is nodding onion, *Allium cernnum,* growing six to 20 inches tall. It has a nodding umbel (meaning all the flower stalks arise at one central point in the flower head) of white or rose flowers. It grows in valleys, on hillsides and up mountains.

All the wild onions have the characteristic smell in the leaves and bulbs.

The Indians made good use of this food plant, as did the early trappers and settlers.

You can use the wild onion to flavor your cooking. But be very careful you don't dig up death-camas by mistake. Wild onion and death-camas and blue camas can grow all together. You must learn to identify death-camas before you dig any bulbs for use.

Chives

Allium schoenoprasum

Wild chives has the same scientific name as garden chives — *Allium schoenoprasum*. That means the plant is the same species.

Chives, onion, garlic, scallions and leeks are all *Allium* genus. They all have a bulb, grass-like leaves and a pungent smell.

Wild chives, also called Siberian chives, has a small elongated bulb and grows in clumps. It is the only wild onion-type plant that has hollow leaves. The other wild onions and wild garlics have solid flat leaves.

The leaves of chives are about a foot high but the flower stem can be two feet high.

The rose or purple-pink blossoms are in a dense flowerhead shaped like a round ball. The plant is found in moist ground from middle altitude to just above timberline. Glacier Park has large patches.

At lower altitude, blooms can be seen in June. At higher altitude, they appear in July and August.

Wild chives is an edible plant. It has a very strong flavor — almost too strong for ordinary taste, at least in the bulb. Campers use the green tops to spice up their food. For real cooking, the wild onion called nodding onion has a much milder taste. You use the bulb of the nodding onion. Be careful in using any wild onion unless you can positively identify the similar death-camas. The leaves and bulbs look very much alike.

The Indians and early settlers probably used the bulbs of all the *Allium* species, including the hot wild chives.

The Blackfeet Indians boiled the bulbs with their meat and also preserved some for later use. Lewis and Clark collected quantities to help out on their meat and root diet.

Wild animals such as bears and ground squirrels dig the bulbs. The green tops are grazed by deer and elk. Cows will graze wild onions and then the milk has an onion taste.

Chives — either the wild variety or the cultivated type — can be planted in the garden as an herb which also serves as a decorative plant. It looks quite pretty in a border with its bright green leaves and clover-like heads of flowers.

You can cut the leaves to use in salads, soups and for seasoning. A chive omelet is a fine dish, also cottage cheese with chives.

The plant is native to Europe, Asia and North America.

Thistle

Common Thistle *(Cirsium vulgare)*

Thistle is a good wilderness emergency food because it grows everywhere and it is easy to identify. There are many different thistles but they are all spiny.

Common thistle, also called bull thistle or spear thistle, is *Cirsium vulgare,* and is an import from Eurasia, now growing widely in North America.

It is a biennial. The first year there is only a flat rosette of spiny leaves. The second year the flowering stalk appears, two to five feet tall, with many branches and large heads of purple or rose flowers.

The rough hairy prickly leaves are lobed like those of the dandelion. The stalks are prickly from top to bottom.

This thistle was known as a potherb in Europe for centuries.

The very young leaves can be eaten raw in a salad but with older leaves you have to remove the spines with a sharp knife and then cook the leaves like spinach.

The young stems can be eaten raw or cooked, first removing the spines.

The part of the thistle that would give you the most food in an emergency is the root. It can be eaten raw or cooked. Use the root of the first-year rosette of leaves.

Some people use the base of the flower, after the bloom has faded, as a sort of "heart of artichoke." The artichoke is a thistle too but it has large flower bases.

For a camp meal, try a fish stuffed with bread crumbs, using peeled, chopped thistle stems instead of your usual celery.

Thistle seeds have long silky hairs or "down" which can be used as tinder to help start a campfire.

In an emergency, a thistle patch is a good place to head for. You have food, you have tinder, and if there is a stream nearby, you can braid a fishline out of the fibers from the thistle stem.

You do not have to be afraid of being poisoned because there is no poisonous plant that looks much like thistle.

The name *Cirsium* comes from the Greek *kirsos* which means a swollen vein. Thistle was reputed to be a remedy for that ailment.

Elk Thistle *(Cirsium scariosum)*

Elk thistle is sometimes called Everts' thistle because it saved the life of Truman Everts, the explorer, when he was lost in Yellowstone National Park in 1870. Having broken his glasses when he was thrown from his horse, he was at a disadvantage in looking for food, but he was

59

near elk thistle *(Cirsium scariosum)* and he lived on the roots until he was found a month later.

Most thistles are edible — leaves, peeled stems, and roots — raw or cooked.

Elk thistle has a thick leafy unbranched stem that can be three feet tall but it can also be only inches tall. The flowerheads cluster in among the leaves at the top of the stem. If the plant is very short, the clustered flowerheads look as if they were sitting on the ground in a rosette of spiny leaves. The color of the flowerheads is pale lilac-purple or white. The spines are weak compared to the stiff prickles of some other thistles.

Elk thistle grows in moist places, from low valleys to rather high up in the mountains. It is eaten — as the name suggests — by elk, and also by bears. Horses will crop it too.

The edible thistle written about by Meriwether Lewis is *C. edule.* The expedition was camped at Fort Clatsop near the mouth of the Columbia and this thistle grew there abundantly. Lewis wrote: "The root of the Thistle, when first taken from the earth, is white and nearly as crisp as a carrot; when prepared for uce, it becomes black, and is more shugary than any fruit or root that I have met with in uce among the natives." They ate it raw sometimes, but generally they roasted it because it was sweeter then.

To agriculturists thistles are a pest. The species named Canada thistle *(C. arvense)* is especially troublesome. It came from Europe and is now widespread and a truly noxious weed.

Burdock

Common Burdock *(Arctium minus)*

Most of us know burdock as a pesky weed, sticking to our clothes, getting in our hair, matting the coats of animals.

It is also an edible plant. It is used wild in many places and has

actually been cultivated in Europe and Asia. In Japan it is used in sukiyaki.

It has a rank taste and must be properly prepared. If you plan to use the early spring growth as a potherb, you have to pick it when very young and parboil it in two waters.

The roots are the part used in sukiyaki, but they must be the roots of the first-year plants, not the second when the flowering stalk develops. Peel the roots and boil in two waters.

These roots can be roasted and ground up to use as a tea or coffee substitute.

The third part of the plant used is the pith of the flowering stalk. Gather the stalks just when the flowerheads are starting to form. Then peel off every bit of the bitter green rind and boil twice. You can follow this oldtime recipe: "the rindle being peeled off...boil in the broth of fat meat."

In Hawaii cultivated burdock roots are sold under the name gobo. Hawaiian natives say eating gobo gives a person strength and endurance.

In herb medicine burdock roots are steeped in water and the infusion was supposed to be good outside for washing burns, wounds and skin irritations, and inside for blood purifying. Burdock beer used to be prepared and was supposed to "cleanse the blood."

Burdock grows along roadsides and in waste places. Since it is a biennial, the first-year growth is a rosette of large dull-green leaves hugging the ground. During the second year, the plant shoots up as high as six feet with a stout stalk, many large leaves, and flowerheads that are generally purple but can be white.

The flowerheads are followed by round seed-burs which fall apart when ripe, a characteristic which makes them doubly hard to remove from clothing and hair.

Burdock is a member of the composite family and is not native to the U.S.A. It came from Europe and Asia.

It is sometimes called clotbur.

Chicory

Cichorium intybus

Chicory is a plant known as a coffee substitute. It is cultivated in Europe and to a limited extent in the United States. Most people know it as a roadside wildflower or weed, more common in the east than in the west.

The flowers are a pretty bright blue and are shaped like a ship's wheel. Perhaps this is why the common name blue-sailors is sometimes used.

Succory is another name, and that came from the scientific name, *Cichorium intybus.*

The flowers open in the morning and close by noon.

The plant grows one to five feet tall, with leaves shaped like a dandelion's and growing in a basal rosette.

People who eat wild plants pick the new young chicory leaves along with new young dandelion leaves. They are both edible. The older leaves of both plants are too bitter to use.

Young chicory roots can be eaten like carrots. The older roots can be roasted and ground for coffee.

Ground roasted chicory root has been used to brew a beverage since ancient times. It is often put in real coffee as an additive. Some people prefer the mixture, saying the chicory adds a special flavor — bitter but rich.

In the old days, chicory was often used as an adulterant for coffee and people drank it without knowing it.

The salad green called endive is closely related to chicory. The scientific name for endive is *Cichorium endivia*. It has a rather bitter taste but many people, especially Europeans, like it.

Chicory can be used in the same way as endive if it is properly grown and blanched. In fact, chicory is sometimes called wild endive.

One variety of chicory grown commercially is Witloof chicory. It has a compact head like celery and is sometimes found in the market under the name of Belgian or French endive.

Chicory is a perennial of the aster or daisy family.

The flower petals can be candied. Charles II, the English king known as the merry monarch, was very fond of the delicacy.

Meadow Salsify

Tragopogon pratensis

Meadow salsify has a flower rather like a dandelion but the plant is much taller — one to four feet. The flower grows singly on its stem, and when the flower goes to seed, the seedhead expands until it is as big as a tennis ball.

You can cut this fluffy seedhead and use it in a dried arrangement.

Salsify is not native to America. It was imported from Europe by the early colonists to use as a root vegetable. One species is cultivated today. The roots look like parsnips but have a more exotic taste. People say the taste is rather like oysters. In fact, salsify is called oysterplant or vegetable oyster.

Salsify requires an even longer growing season than parsnips to develop a good fleshy root.

Oysterplant salsify has a purple flower. The salsifies commonly found in the wild have yellow flowers.

The Indians used the salsify plants as food — both the roots and the new young shoots. The milky juice, which coagulates into a gum and can

be chewed, was used as a remedy for indigestion. The juice is quite bitter and would not appeal except as medicine.

The scientific name is *Tragopogon*. *Trago* is from the Greek for goat and *pogon* means beard. A common name for salsify is goat's-beard.

The white seedheads break up into individual seeds that float on the wind like little umbrellas or parachutes.

If you look at one of the seeds under a magnifying glass, you will see how similar the design is to that of an umbrella or parachute or shuttlecock.

Look for meadow salsify in fields, along roadsides, and in waste places. It grows in cities in empty lots. The flowering season is summer but the seedheads can remain into fall.

Camas

Camassia quamash

From late April to mid-June, camas will flower in wet meadows in wide expanses that look like blue lakes.

Camas is a lily, the famous blue lily of the Indians and early settlers. To us it is a beautiful flower. To the western Indians and pioneers it was "number one food plant." It was so important it caused wars.

Camassia quamash is the botanical name. Common names include camash and blue camass. The plant has one spike of blue-purble flowers, one to two feet tall, and grasslike leaves. The seed is in short dry pods.

The flowers have three blue petals and three blue sepals all looking

alike. There are about five species of *Camassia*, all in North America.

The onionlike bulb of *Camassia quamash* is white on the inside, black on the outside. It is small. The largest is only an inch in diameter. It seems hard to believe that the Indians, using only digging sticks, could gather enough for a staple food supply. Yet we read in the Lewis and Clark journals that at times the entire expedition lived on camas.

The camas bulb can be eaten raw, dried, boiled, baked or roasted. In the "interests of science" I baked three tiny bulbs in the oven. I had to improvise a cooking method in order to follow more or less the oldtime Indian method. According to the journals, the Indians dug a deep hole in the ground and lined it with heated rocks and grass. The bulbs were laid in the hole in layers separated by layers of grass. A layer of earth covered the hole and then a fire was built on top. Three days and three nights later the pit was opened and the cooked bulbs were spread in the sun to dry.

The dried bulbs could be stored or bartered for other goods.

The books say that the three-day cooking produced a sticky sweet syrup oozing out of the bulbs. The name camas is a corruption of the Nootka Indian word "chamas" which means sweet.

My three bulbs baked in the oven were not sticky and sweet. They were bland and rather gummy. They stuck to my teeth. I had put them in a tiny covered pyrex dish and then set this dish in a larger covered pyrex in which I was baking carrots. The theory was to provide a "pit lined with grass." Of course I did not have the oven on three days and three nights. But I could see there would be good food value in the bulbs.

Some Indian tribes added insects to the bulbs. In California a tribe mixed boiled camas bulbs with a paste of crushed grasshoppers. In Idaho, ants, cooked or roasted, were added.

Gathering camas bulbs can be dangerous. Even the Indians sometimes made mistakes. The deadly poisonous death-camas looks much like blue camas, in both the bulb and the leaves. The flowers are different — death-camas is white or cream-colored — but it seems the Indians dug the bulbs just after the blossoms fell.

You can judge the far-reaching importance of camas as food when you consider there are places named after the plant in Idaho, Montana, Washington, Utah and Oregon. Also Fort Victoria on Vancouver Island was once called Camosun or "place for gathering camas."

I do not advocate eating camas bulbs. In an emergency, yes, but this beautiful lily would soon be extinct if we started digging it for food. We are a nation of 215 million people. We need the shining blue camas meadows to fill our spirit, not our stomach.

Bitterroot

Lewisia rediviva

Bitterroot is the famous plant that was a food staple for the Lewis and Clark expedition in 1805 and 1806. The explorers learned the value of the plant from the Indians who considered it next to the camas in importance. The Indians migrated with their whole encampments to the mountains in May to gather a year's supply.

You can read that "a bag of dried bitterroot was worth as much as a horse." But don't get enthusiastic about heading for the hills to gather a year's supply.

We don't gather the bitterroot at all today. It is so scarce many people living right in Montana, the home of the bitterroot, have never seen it

growing in the wild.

The plant is in the purslane family. The genus is *Lewisia,* named after Captain Meriwether Lewis.

The flower has 12 to 18 petals, white to pink, and no leaves. The leaves come early and wither before the flowers open. The long slender reddish-colored conical buds are characteristic also. The flower is quite large, one to two inches broad, and very showy. Another common name is rockrose.

If you see the plant in its natural habitat, on a stony slope of a bare mountainside, seeming to grow right out of the rocks, you can see why the name rockrose is appropriate.

The plant blooms in May and June. Its special habitat is Montana — it is the state flower — but you can find it north to Canada and south to California, Colorado and Utah.

The Indians gathered the roots before the flowers opened. This is because the roots are most tender and nutritious then and the dark peeling, which is very bitter, can be scraped off easily. After peeling, you have a small clump of thin white roots which can be cooked like spaghetti. The content is almost pure starch so the result of boiling is a jellylike consistency.

But there will always be a reminder of the name — bitter root. You can throw away the first water but you will still have an aftertaste.

The roots were made into meal by drying and then powdering.

This food plant was so important in its day that the name was given to a mountain range, a river and a valley.

Lewis and Clark ate bitterroot while on their expedition and they collected specimens to bring to Washington.

The species name *rediviva,* meaning "brought to life," comes from the experience the botanist Frederick Pursh had with the roots several years later. He looked at the roots and it seemed to him there was a hint of life so he planted some. The roots grew and flowered. These original plants are still alive today — growing and flowering in the Philadelphia Academy of Sciences.

The Kew Botanical Gardens in England grew plants from roots that had been immersed in boiling water and stored in the herbarium for a year and a half.

Then why is it so hard to find the state flower of Montana, you might well ask.

The answer is civilization. The habitat gets squeezed. There are more people and fewer undisturbed areas.

Springbeauty

Western Springbeauty *(Claytonia lanceolata)*

I don't recommend eating springbeauty. It is a pretty early-spring wildflower and we need it more to admire than to put in the stewpot.

Both the green leaves and the underground tubers, technically called corms, are edible and in an emergency can be used raw or cooked.

The corms are tiny, about the size of a cherry. The Indians used them as a staple food. They look and taste like potatoes but when would we consider potatoes the size of cherries as a staple food. It shows how hard the Indians worked to gather their food.

68

You can spot springbeauty as early as April, often growing right near a snowbank. It has two opposite leaves and white to pink flowers, generally five-petaled. The petals are veined in darker pink. The plant is small, only six to eight inches tall.

It is in the same family, the purslane, as bitterroot. In fact, there is an alpine species of springbeauty that is often confused with the alpine pygmy bitterroot.

Springbeauty grows in moist soil in valleys, mountain parks and along the edge of woods. Varieties are found in both the eastern and western United States. The names groundnut and fairy spud are used in some localities.

Grizzly bears eat the corms. In grizzly habitat you sometimes see gaping holes in the middle of a springbeauty patch.

Glacier Lily

Erythronium grandiflorum

The bulb, really a corm, of glacier lily is buried deep in the ground. It is edible and has a mild taste but it should be used only in an emergency. Any flower that can bloom through a snowbank deserves admiration, not depletion. Grizzly bears eat the corms but we have to concede them that privilege.

The green leaves can be used raw in salad but try them in a small quantity as some people have found they have a laxative effect.

The seed pods can be eaten raw or cooked. It is easy to find enough seed pods to make a cooked vegetable and you do no harm to the perennial root.

The bulbs have been known as food for centuries. Oldtime American Indians used them boiled fresh, or dried for winter use. In Eurasia the ancient Tartars boiled the bulbs of a purple-flowered glacier lily in broth or milk.

There are no purple-flowered species in the United States. There are yellow and white ones.

Grandiflorum means large-flowered. The Rocky Mountain glacier lilies are large and they are quite fragile looking. That is why it comes as rather a surprise to be hiking up a mountain with an icy wind in one's face and suddenly come upon a bright yellow lily growing at the edge of a glacier.

One ought to write a poem to the glacier lily. Blooming at the edge of perpetual snow, it survives mountain blasts yet looks as delicate as a hothouse plant.

Glacier lily has so many names it is confusing. Dogtooth violet, for instance, is one of the common names. But this plant is not a violet. It is a lily. The scientific name is *Erythronium grandiflorum* and the family is *liliaceae.*

Snow lily is another common name. This one is appropriate because you often see a bright yellow bloom coming right through snow.

The name fawn lily is appropriate for several reasons. The flowers start to bloom when fawns are being born and also the two leaves of the plant stand up with the alert look of a fawn's ears.

The eastern species, *E. americanum,* has mottled leaves and some wildflower enthusasts say the name fawn lily could come from the similarity to a fawn's speckled hide.

Trout lily is another name that could be traced to the eastern species' mottled leaves. Or it could be traced to the season and the habitat. A good clear trout stream quite often tumbles along between banks covered with the lily.

The derivation of the name adder's tongue is not too clear. Does it come from the markings of the leaves or do the petals curve in a way that suggests a snake's tongue?

It is fun to try to figure out why flowers were given their common names. We say "vulgar" names in botany but we don't mean vulgar in the uncouth sense. Originally vulgar meant "in general use."

Glacier lily starts to bloom at lower elevations in April. At higher elevations it is only starting in July and August. If you are a hiker, you often find that midsummer flowers are blooming in the valley, then, as you climb up the mountain, you are back in spring and if you climb high enough, you are back in winter and there are no flowers at all.

Yellow Bell

Fritillaria pudica

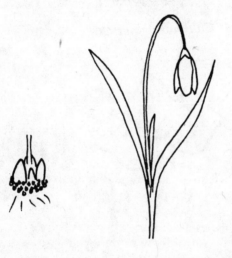

Yellow bell has an edible bulb but it is not plentiful enough to advocate using it as food.

It is in the lily family and the bloom is sometimes confused with glacier lily. However, the petals of yellow bell do not curve backward. The yellow bell-like flower hangs on a nodding stem, a characteristic which goes with the scientific name *pudica,* meaning shy.

The bell is formed by three sepals and three petals, but the sepals look so much like the petals that the flower simply looks like six yellow petals.

The plant is small, about six inches tall. It blooms in early spring, sometimes in March at lower elevations. At higher altitudes it blooms in May and June. The flower is chrome yellow at first then changes to orange-red with age.

There are several species. Yellow bell, also called yellow fritillary, is the most common. The purple-flowered *F. atropurpurea,* called leopard lily, is a larger plant but scarcer.

Both species were used by the Indians. The starchy bulb is surrounded by tiny bulblets like grains of rice. In fact, rice-root is a common name for the species, *F. lanceolata*.

The Alaskan *F. camschatcensis*, or Kamtchatka lily, is called Indian rice. The bulbs are still used today: fresh, dried, or made into flour.

The green seed pods of any of the species can be eaten raw in salad or boiled as a vegetable.

Sego Lily

Calochortus nuttallii

If you were lost and starving, you could dig sego lily bulbs and cook them. The Indians and early settlers used these bulbs as we do potatoes.

Sego lily became the state flower of Utah because it saved the life of a great many Mormon settlers during the famine years around 1850. There was a serious shortage of food at that time due to drought and hordes of grasshoppers.

It was no easy job to gather enough sego lily bulbs to feed hundreds of people. The bulb is tiny, about an inch in diameter, and it is set deep and tight in the ground. It is really a hardship food. Can you imagine how we moderns would feel if the markets suddenly carried a supply of potatoes one inch in diameter?

The Indians and pioneers roasted or baked the tiny bulbs or dried them and ground them into meal called sago. A kind of bread was sometimes made from the meal.

The flower looks like a white triangular tulip. It also looks like a white butterfly sitting in a field. This accounts for some of the other common names: star tulip, butterfly tulip, mariposa lily. Mariposa means butterfly in Spanish.

The three large white petals dotted or banded with purple at the base do look like a butterfly's wings. The three sepals under the petals help form a sort of star. The flower grows from 8 to 20 inches high and has a few grasslike leaves.

You find sego lily blooming in June and July on dry open ground or on hillsides and gravelly slopes. There are nine species in the Rockies, mostly white or cream-colored. In California there is a bright orange variety.

The family is *Liliaceae* and the genus is *Calochortus,* which means pretty grass. The species name honors the botanist Thomas Nuttall.

Sego lily should not be considered a source of food. It is edible but it is not abundant. The bulbs should be left to produce the lovely flowers.

Wild Hyacinth

Brodiaea douglasii

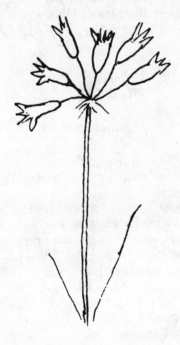

Wild hyacinth, like sego lily, has an edible bulb but the plant is not common enough to be a source of food.

73

It was used by the Indians and early settlers and has a good flavor, raw or cooked. Gophernuts is one of the names given to the bulbs.

Technically brodiaea bulbs are corms because they are solid. Bulbs are supposed to be made up of scales like an onion.

The young seed pods are also edible and can be cooked like a vegetable. But don't picture a dish heaped with succulent green pods like Oriental snow peas or green beans. The wild hyacinth pod is the length of our fingernail. You would be using the seed production of a whole hillside to make a family serving of vegetable.

Wild hyacinth grows like wild onion and blue camas. They all have grasslike leaves and are in the lily family.

Wild hyacinth is not really a hyacinth. It is a brodiaea. The brodiaeas have their flowers in an umbel like wild onion. To tell the brodiaeas from the onions look at the formation of the flowers. The brodiaeas have the petals fused into a tube.

Brodiaea douglasii has lilac-blue flowers, sometimes pale, sometimes dark. The number of flowers in the umbel varies from a few to to as many as 25. The stalks are leafless and from one to three feet tall.

The plants bloom in May and June and grow in meadows, open woods and rocky hillsides. They often grow in patches and make a pretty showing. If we want to enjoy their lovely blue color it's best we leave the eating to the animals.

Red Lily

Lilium philadelphicum

Red lily is so bright a scarlet that in spots where it is plentiful, it looks like goblets of fire.

The trouble is there aren't many spots where this beautiful brilliant flower survives. An old-time botanist wrote "Sometimes lilies are so abundant that they cover an acre of ground bright red."

Many of us have never seen red lily, also called wood lily. It grows in mountain meadows, open woods and thickets.

The plant is one to two feet tall and has leafy stems. The six-petaled, cup-shaped flowers are fire-red, spotted with dark purple. There can be from one to three flowers on a stem.

The generally accepted scientific name is *Lilium philadelphicum*. There is an eastern variety and a western variety.

Many lily species are edible. Red lily bulbs were used by the Indians.

Early travelers used them as a substitute for potatoes but they did not rave about the taste. An old diary says the bulbs were so bitter they ruined the "rubaboo" which was a stew made of boiled pemmican thickened with flour.

I hope none of us would dream of eating the red lily. It is too scarce. We have to leave the few that are left so that when we hike in the mountains, once in a while we will come upon these spots of red-hot sun.

If you feel like trying lily bulbs, there is an edible one right in your garden — the day-lily. You can eat the buds, the flowers and the underground tubers.

The day-lily often escapes from gardens and establishes itself in the wild.

Bistort

American Bistort (Polygonum bistortoides)

Once you have learned to distinguish American bistort (Polygonum bistortoides), you have a good emergency wild food. The rootstock is starchy and thus has nutritional value.

Species of bistort have been eaten in Europe and Asia for centuries. In

North America the Indians used the roots raw, roasted, or boiled in the soup or stew which generally formed the main dish of the Indian meal.

American bistort, also called Western bistort or snakeweed, has leaves like some of the docks, which is not surprising because bistort is also in the buckwheat family.

The leaves can be boiled and eaten. They have a tart taste like curly dock or sheep sorrel.

The flower spike appears in June or July and looks rather like a white or pinkish-white tuft of cotton on a slender unbranched stem half a foot to two and a half feet high.

The flower cluster, when white, could be mistaken for one of the death-camas species by a beginner outdoorsman, so look at the leaves of both plants and get them firmly in mind. The two plants sometimes grow side by side on hillsides, flowering at the same time.

There are many species of *Polygonum,* some being other bistorts, some being knotweeds, smartweeds or lady's-thumbs.

The name snakeweed for *P. bistortoides* could have originated from either the shape of the root or from their use. An old book says: "The roote of Bistorte is knobbie or bunched, crookedly turned or writhed this way and that way, whereof it took his name Bistorta. The iuyce prevaileth much against the biting of Serpents and other venomous Beastes."

The use of certain species of bistort as a cure for snakebite was known both in Europe and among the Northwest Indians.

The smaller bistort found in the Rockies is *P. viviparum.* It is also edible and is called by the common names alpine bistort, viviparous bistort and sometimes European bistort. This species produces bulblets on the flower stem, hence the name viviparous.

Jerusalem Artichoke

Helianthus tuberosus

Jerusalem artichoke is not an artichoke and it did not come from Jerusalem. It is a sunflower, growing in the style of the ordinary wild sunflowers.

The roots are the important part, not the seeds. The roots are like small knobby potatoes and can be eaten raw or cooked. They are easily digested and are used in certain dietary preparations.

The plant is native to North America. It was taken from here to Europe and cultivated there. It is used in parts of Europe as a cooked vegetable and also as a livestock feed.

The tubers are tan or brown on the outside, white on the inside. They are crisp like a turnip and will stay crisp if kept in the ground or in the refrigerator in a plastic bag, but if dug like potatoes and left in the open air, they will shrivel.

The plant grows three to ten feet tall. The rough leaves are toothed and end in a sharp point. There are many yellow flowers on slender stems. The flowers do not have the large brown disk of the sunflower we grow for the seeds. Flowering season is late summer.

Adventurous gardeners can enjoy raising a patch of Jerusalem artichokes. They are easy to grow and the tubers can be left in the ground all winter.

All you need to start a patch is one tuber. Cut it into chunks, leaving one "eye" in each chunk and plant. The following fall you will have a harvest.

When you want to use a tuber, dig it out of the ground. It is tasty in a raw salad — sweet and crisp and juicy.

The Indians used both the Jerusalem artichoke and the common sunflower as food.

The scientific name for Jerusalem artichoke is *Helianthus tuberosus*. It is sometimes called girasole which is Italian for sunflower. The Spanish word is almost the same — *girasol*.

Cooked Jerusalem artichokes are best boiled or cooked along with a roast in the oven. They can be mashed but they get watery instead of creamy.

They can be pickled. Simply boil them, then store in vinegar.

Some people peel the tubers, others like the taste skin and all.

Balsamroot

Arrowleaf Balsamroot *(Balsamorhiza sagittata)*

Arrowleaf balsamroot may look like a sunflower but it is not. You can tell arrowleaf balsamroot by the bunches of large silvery arrow-shaped leaves and the almost leafless flower stalks rising from the clump. The flower stalks have a silvery appearance also, due to a dense mat of woolly hairs.

This perennial herb is in the composite family — *Compositae*. This is the daisy family and the flowers are characterized by the fact that what looks like a single flower is really a "composite" of complete disk flowers (the center) and complete ray flowers (the outside).

Arrowleaf balsamroot colors whole hillsides golden yellow from late April to early July. When the yellow balsamroot is mixed with purple lupine, the hillsides are really striking.

The scientific name for arrowleaf balsamroot is *Balsamorhiza sagittata*. *Balsamorhiza* comes from the Greek word *balsamon* meaning balsam and *rhiza* for root. This name is very logical because the thick tuberous root of this genus has a dark resinous cover that tastes like balsam.

There are about a dozen species of *Balsamorhiza*, found mostly in western North America. *Sagittata* means arrow-leaved. Another common species is *B. hookeri,* sometimes given the common name balsamroot. This one is not arrow-leaved. It has incised leaves. Incised means cut sharply and irregularly.

You can tell the balsamroots from another yellow spring bloomer, heartleaf arnica, by the fact that arnica is smaller and the plant is not a clump. It grows in patches like the glacier lilies do, and each plant has only one flower stalk.

The flowerhead of arrowleaf balsamroot is two to four inches across. The stalks are from six inches to two feet tall.

This plant was a very important food in the old days of Indians and fur trappers. Some authorities put this plant third in importance, the first being camas and the second being bitterroot.

The seeds were ground into flour and made into a sort of biscuit. In some areas, it was so popular it became known as Mormon biscuit. The flour was called pinole.

The young tender spring leaves made a juicy salad. The Indians peeled the roots of their potent balsam rind and then the center was white and when added to stew was mealy and edible.

The leaves were used by the Blackfeet in their Sun Dance ceremony. They cooked them along with the sacred camas bulbs.

We would find the plant bitter. If you wish to try making flour, dig the roots in early spring and parboil before drying and grinding.

The leaves are edible only when very young. The stems of the flowers can be peeled and chewed on like celery. The taste will be bitter.

Wild Carrot

Daucus carota

Wild carrot is Queen Anne's lace and it is the ancestor of our garden carrot.

The scientific name for both garden and wild carrot is *Daucus carota*. You could dig the root of Queen Anne's lace and eat it.

You would probably find it small and stringy, and you would be ready to thank the scientists for developing our sweet succulent garden carrot from those humble beginnings.

Wild carrot is sometimes listed as a "poisonous" plant. This is because the plant causes dermatitis in some people, and the bitter tops, when eaten by cows, cause bitter-tasting milk.

In addition, we have to remember wild carrot is in the parsley family which has the deadly water-hemlock and poison-hemlock. We have to be very careful when using any member of this family.

Therefore, even though the Indians used the roots of wild carrot and it could be an emergency food, it is best we consider it only as a roadside wildflower, rather pretty with its lacy foliage and its lacy umbels of white flowers.

It grows from six inches to three feet tall, along roadsides and in waste places. It is considered by farmers a weed and in some parts is called devil's plague.

Bird's-nest is another common name and that refers to the curled-up cuplike form the flower umbel assumes after the individual blossoms wither.

Some people have used wild carrot seeds for sprouting and have dried the leaves for use as a salt substitute. In the old days, when people did not know about allergies or had tougher digestive systems, the younger shoots and roots were pickled, and the older roots were dried and roasted for a coffee substitute.

The carrot in its cultivated beginnings was sometimes used as an herb medicine. Grated raw, it was made into a poultice for "blacke and bleu spots that come of dry beatings."

But it was also a food and probably prepared much as we use it today. According to an early writer, this vegetable gives great pleasure "Boyled in the broth of beefe..."

Biscuit-root

Cous Biscuit-root *(Lomatium cous)*

When Lewis and Clark wrote that they ate bread of "cows," they were talking about cous biscuit-root, or *Lomatium cous.*

There are many Lomatiums all looking much alike and generally called desert parsley because they are in the parsley family and grow in dry areas.

There are several edible desert parsleys. The French Canadians called the root *racine blanche* and the Indians knew it as cous or cows.

Some of the biscuit-roots have yellow flowers, some have white, and a few have purple. The flowers look somewhat like Queen Anne's lace — a filigreed umbrella head. The leaves are finely dissected like those of carrot. The smell and taste of the leaves is that of parsley.

The roots are thick and fleshy and that is the cous or cows of the Indians.

The Indians gathered large amounts of the roots and used them as food and trade.

Lewis and Clark bought their biscuit-root from the Indians. One of the journal entries describes such a transaction: "One of our men to-day brought home three bushels of roots and some bread of Cows which in one situation, was as important as the return of an East Indian ship."

According to another writer, it was wise to buy the roots from the Indians instead of digging them because there are several members of the parsley family which are poisonous — water-hemlock and poison-hemlock.

We moderns, accustomed to white bread and the bland Irish potato, might not find biscuit-root a very palatable dish. Lewis wrote: "We still place our chief reliance on the mush made of roots (amongst these the Cows and Quamash are the principle) with which we use a small onion which grows in great abundance, and which corrects any bad effects they may have on our stomach."

The bicuit-root could be eaten raw, where it had a taste like celery, but usually it was ground into a flour and made into bread in the form of large flat cakes.

Today the use of the roots is mostly left to bears, gophers and mice.

Yampah

Perideridia gairdneri

Yampah is one of the tastier wild foods. The roots are like parsnips but better. The drawback to eating yampah (also spelled yampa) is that identification is difficult. There are dozens of plants that look like yampah. It is not conspicuous or distinct. And the very poisonous water-hemlock and poison-hemlock are in the same family.

There are three species of yampah in the west. A common one is Gairdner's yampah —*Perideridia gairdneri*. It grows from one to three

82

feet tall, usually solitary. The leaves are divided into narrow grasslike leaflets.

The blossoms are dainty white flowerheads in the characteristic umbels of the parsley family. Queen Anne's lace has flowers like this, also the biscuit-roots, cow-parsnip, and the poisonous water-hemlock and poison-hemlock.

The plant grows in damp soil in meadows, on hillsides and in woodland.

The roots were an important food for the Indians and early settlers. There is a river, a valley and a town in northwestern Colorado all named after the plant. The name Yampah was once considered for the state of Colorado.

The Indians used the roots raw, boiled, or as flour. The raw root is white, firm and crisp. It can be dried and pounded into a white meal which is easy to digest. Indian mothers used it to feed their children.

Yampah is sometimes called squaw root but that name can refer to many plants.

False-caraway is another name and that refers to the seeds which have been used for seasoning. They remind you of the true caraway seeds.

The Indians gathered the roots in the fall. By that time the leaves are withered and dried up.

If you are going to collect yampah tubers for eating, you will have to be very careful.

Sedge

Nebraska Sedge *(Carex nebrascenis)*

Sedge looks like grass and is not at all conspicuous but in an emergency you could eat the young shoots and also the underground stems. Some species form tubers called "ground nuts."

Sedge grows in wet soil — meadows, bogs, stream-banks.

There are about 100 species in the Rockies. To tell one sedge from another is very difficult but at least you can say "This is a sedge" if you remember that sedge has a solid stem which is triangular in shape. Most grasses have round hollow stems.

Sedge is much more noticeable at high altitude because there are not so many other plants there. At low altitude sedge mixes with the grasses.

Sedges do well in the cold wet arctic and alpine regions.

Some of the sedge species have the flower spikes erect, others have

drooping spikes.

Nebraska sedge, *Carex nebrascensis,* is a common western species. The leaves and stem are blue-green and the flower spikes are dark-colored. The plant can be less than a foot tall or it can be three feet tall. There can be only two flower spikes or as many as six.

The flower spikes are in bloom in mid-summer.

You can pull a sedge at any time and nibble the base of the stem. This is a favorite food of muskrats, bears and elk. In fact, one of the sedges is called elk sedge.

Silverweed

Potentilla anserina

Silverweed is an edible cinquefoil. The roots can be eaten like parsnips.

Silverweed, also called goosegrass or goose tansy, is a spreading plant growing in the manner of wild strawberry, sending out runners to establish new plants. The plant is low-growing but the runners can be two feet long.

The leaves are fern-like and silky, usually green above, silvery-white underneath. There can be as many as 31 leaflets.

The flowers are five-petaled, bright yellow, blooming May to July.

The plant grows in wet soil and is often found in farm pastures, but it will also grow at altitudes up to 8,000 feet. It can survive in poor soil.

It is native to Eurasia but has spread to many parts of the world and has often served as a food mainstay in times of famine. In western

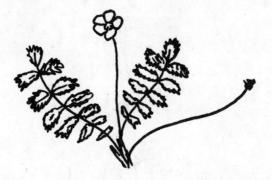

Scotland it once kept the entire population alive. The popular name for the roots was moors.

The Indians here in North America used the roots boiled or roasted. They can also be eaten raw, and that is why the plant is listed as an excellent survival food. It is also easily identified.

The raw roots taste all right — starchy, rather pleasantly nutty. When cooked they look like parsnips but they are crisper and not as sweet. They have a mild taste.

However, don't expect too much of silverweed. The roots are pencil-thin and hard to dig. You would have to work to get a meal.

The name *anserina* means "of geese" and refers to the plant being eaten by geese. The genus *Potentilla* is the five-finger genus.

Tobacco-root

Valeriana edulis

Tobacco-root is edible valerian and it was a valuable food of the Indians but I would not recommend it. Raw, it is considered to be poisonous and even when cooked in the Indian way — the roots were baked in the ground for two days — the smell and taste can only be compared to chewing tobacco.

There are about a dozen valerians in the United States. Tobacco-root is *Valeriana edulis*. It is a perennial growing four to 24 inches tall. The small flowers are whitish or cream-colored. The leaves are opposite and can be entire or divided.

The roots grow like a carrot and can be quite large. Some of the Indians tribes used this plant a great deal, even with its "strong and remarkably peculiar taste and odor," as the explorer, J. C. Fremont, wrote.

Nevertheless, he ate it. As he said, "I was afterward always glad when

85

it formed an addition to our scanty meals."

That is the secret of many wild foods. If they are an addition to "scanty" meals, they begin to taste a little better.

In an emergency, you could dig the roots and maybe boil them in many changes of water or bake in the ashes for hours. But you would probably do better to concentrate on another source of food.

Some of the valerians have a medicinal reputation. *V. officinalis* is a European species which is cultivated for the drug valerian. This plant is sometimes grown in gardens as an ornamental, called garden heliotrope or garden valerian. It is not a true heliotrope.

Indian Bread-root

Psoralea esculenta

What Lewis and Clark called a "kind of ground potato" when they talked about being camped in Montana and being invited to an Indian feast which "consisted of cooked dog, pemetigon and a kind of ground potato...placed before us in platters with horn spoons." they meant not what we mean by a potato but the root of a prairie plant — *Psoralea esculenta* — which is in the pea family and has enlarged roots rather like the tubers of a dahlia.

Lewis and Clark thought the "potato" was good, and said it was cooked "dressed like the preparation of corn called hominy, to which it is little inferior."

It was a staple item among the food of the prairie Indians and trappers and they gave it many names: Indian bread, bread-root, prairie turnip, prairie potato.

The taste is described as halfway between a potato and a turnip, a little sweet. The food content is starch and sugar.

John Colter, the mountain man, once lived for a week largely on this root.

The tubers are only one and a half to two inches long so it takes work to dig a good supply. The tubers can be eaten raw, roasted or dried in the sun and ground up for flour.

The plant looks like a lupine. It has blue clover-like flowers on short dense spikes. It has five leaflets which are smooth above and hairy underneath. Both leaves and stems are covered with black scurfy dots which give the plant its botanic name. *Psoralea* comes from a Greek work meaning mange and refers to the scabs on the plant. Scurf-pea is another common name.

The plant is a perennial. The erect stems are from six to 18 inches tall. The stalks mature early and break off in the wind so amateur hunters would have to start digging the roots in early summer in order to know what they were digging.

The root called Indian potato in eastern U.S. is *Apios americana,* also in the pea family, also tasting somewhat turnip-like, but the plant is a vine growing in the form of garden bean or pea. The part used is the underground tubers which are small enough to be commonly called ground nuts. The Pilgrims were introduced to this food by friendly

Indians and it was a mainstay of their diet during their first winter in Plymouth.

If we did not have the large Irish potato as a cultivated vegetable we would likely experiment with growing some of the wild "potatoes."

Wild Licorice

Glycyrrhiza lepidota

Licorice is a flavor and a candy but it is also a plant.

The licorice plant that produces the commercial product does not grow wild in the U.S.A. but our native species has the same flavor and could be used if necessary.

The native species is *Glycyrrhiza lepidota* and is called American licorice or licorice-root. It is in the pea family and is a coarse weedy plant growing one to three feet tall. It has greenish-white flowers and leaves that are compound like those of a locust tree or mountain ash. The leaves are spotted with small scurfy dots — hence the name *lepidota*.

The plant grows in patches along ditches and in foothills. The flowers open in summer. The seed pods are brown prickly burs which can be a nuisance when they get in the wool of sheep.

There are several species of licorice. Most have the characteristic sweet, licorice-flavored juice.

The word *Glycyrrhiza* is a corruption of the Greek name *Glykyrrhiza* meaning sweet root. The roots of American licorice are thicker than the other species and can be roasted like sweet potatoes and used for food. Lewis and Clark wrote the following description: "The lickrice here grows verry abundant and large; the natives roste it in the embers and pound it Slightly with a Small Stick in order to make it Seperate more readily from the Strong liggaments which forms the Center of the root; this they discard, and chew and Swallow the ballance of the root."

Some early settlers said the roasted roots tasted all right. Others found them too astringent.

The licorice of commerce comes from *G. glabra* which is native to southern Europe. It is cultivated there and also in parts of the United States, especially California and Louisiana. The long thin roots are crushed, boiled and the water is evaporated.

Licorice was used as a cough-remedy as far back as the third century B.C. In old England the herbal books listed the value of licorice as "It openeth the pipes of the lunges when they be stuffed or stopt."

Sweet-cicely

Western Sweet-cicely *(Osmorhiza occidentalis)*

This plant with a name like a girl's has the flavor of anise or licorice and can be used in cooking.

The name sweet-cicely can refer to several plants of the parsley family. The common sweet-cicely is in the *Osmorhiza* genus, and has a ferny leaf and flat-topped umbels (clusters) of usually yellowish or greenish-white flowers. It grows to three and a half feet tall, generally in lightly shaded woodland.

The narrow tapering seeds cling to clothes and hair.

All parts of the plant have the anise flavor. The fresh leaves can be used or the seeds or the roots.

Commercial licorice is obtained from a different genus of plants — the *Glycyrrhiza* of the pea family. There are quite a few plants of very different genera that have anise or licorice flavor.

Sweet-cicely can be used to make anise cookies. Dry the roots, then scrape or pound them into a powder. If you want a strong anise flavor, add the powder to the cookie dough. If you want the milder flavor, make a tea of the powder and use only the strained tea.

The roots can be boiled and eaten like parsnips. The anise flavor is there but in an emergency you might not mind it.

Osmorhiza occidentalis, called western sweet-root, has a strong flavor.

The difficulty with trying to use any of the *Osmorhiza* genus as food is that these plants can be confused with poison-hemlock and water-hemlock. The parsley family has many edible members — the carrot, parsnip, garden parsley — and such wild plants as biscuit-root, yampah, and wild carrot but it also has poisonous ones.

Arrowhead

Sagittaria cuneata

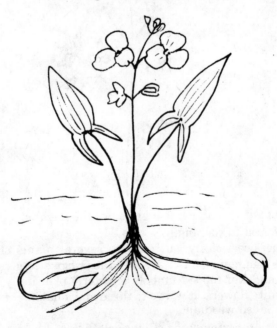

Arrowhead is a water plant that has small potato-like tubers at the ends of the perennial rootstocks. These tubers are nourishing and can be used boiled or roasted. The Indians and early settlers considered arrowhead, or wapato, as it was called, a valuable food plant.

It grows in ponds, at the edges of sluggish rivers, and in marshes. It is found throughout North America, from sea level to mountains. There are about 20 species.

The plant has arrowshaped leaves and three-petaled white flowers.

The tubers average an inch in diameter, rarely becoming larger than the size of an egg. They are bitter when raw but when cooked, they can take the place of potatoes.

Lewis and Clark used these "swamp potatoes" as a staple food supply during their voyage to the Pacific. In the expedition journal Clark wrote: "Wappatoe grows in great abundance in the marshy grounds of that butifull and fertile Vally on the Columbia...this bulb forms a principal article of traffic between the inhabitents of the Vally and those of the sea coast."

The task of gathering the tubers was undertaken by the Indian women. It was not easy. The tubers grow under water and then under dirt, sometimes a foot under. The Indian women waded into the water, sometimes breast-deep, pushing a canoe ahead of them. They felt around in the mud and dirt at the bottom with their toes until they located the tubers, then they loosened the tubers and let them float to the surface, where later they could be gathered and put in the canoe.

The tubers are the largest in the fall so that is a good gathering time. Of course the water is not at its warmest. If the water is not too deep, wading in hip boots would be the modern way to gather the tubers. Be prepared to search, as the tubers can be several feet from the main stalk of the plant.

The Indians prepared the tubers by boiling them in wooden kettles with hot stones put into the water or by roasting. Roasting was done by two methods: on sticks stuck in the ground near the fire, or in stone-lined kilns. The boiled tubers could be preserved for winter by slicing and drying.

Modern ways to prepare arrowhead are as "potato" salad, baked in foil, fried or boiled. An Oriental touch is to use arrowhead tubers as a substitute for water chestnuts, in Chinese and Japanese dishes. True water chestnuts come from the Orient but even there *Sagittaria* is used. It is actually cultivated.

Muskrats store the tubers in their nests. The Indians sometimes stole these caches.

Flour can be made from boiled, dried tubers.

Cow-lily

Nuphar polysepalum

Cow-lily, also called yellow water-lily, is an edible plant. In an emergency, you could eat the big rootstocks. They are not especially delicious as they have a strong flavor but you could boil them in two or three changes of water and then the flavor is not so pronounced.

This plant grows in lakes, ponds, or slow streams. The large leaves, up to a foot or more in length, are oval or round and may be floating on the surface or held above it.

The large cup-like waxy flowers are golden yellow, sometimes tinged with red.

The scientific name is *Nuphar polysepalum*, the *Nuphar* coming from the Arabic word for some water lily.

The water-lily family name is *Nymphaeaceae*, coming from the Greek word for water nymph.

Other common names for cow-lily are spatterdock, Indian pond lily and wakas or wokas.

Wokas is what the Indians called the seeds. These large seeds can be roasted, then shelled and ground or pounded into a meal.

The Klamath Indians considered cow-lily seeds a staple food. The harvest entailed the use of canoes as cow-lilies grow in four or five feet of water. The pods were picked by hand if they were still on the plant. If they were floating on the water they were scooped up with a wicker spoon.

In order to separate the seeds, the pods were put in holes in the ground, where they fermented into a sticky mass and then the seeds could be washed out.

The roots were used mostly in times of famine. The Indians made meal by slicing and drying the huge roots and then grinding them.

If we want to try the meal, we would probably soak it in several changes of water in order to remove some of the strong taste.

We would not find it easy to gather the roots. They are buried in mud at the bottom of the river or pond. The Indians often raided muskrat houses. Muskrats gather the roots and store them for winter.

The roots are yellow and scaly and they twist along the pond floor.

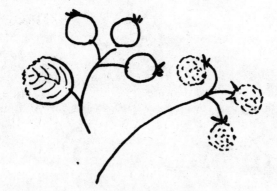

Fruit is Dessert and a Harvest to put by for Winter

Wild fruit is the crowning glory of edible wild plants — both literally and figuratively. It is a bounteous display that attracts our eye and it is also the part of the plant that is the easiest to use, the most plentiful and usually the most nutritious. Bears get fat on wild fruit. Birds feast on it.

You do no harm to plants by using the fruit. In fact, you do the plant a favor because you help scatter the seeds.

Wild fruit is a free harvest but courtesy should be practiced in gathering it. If the fruit is on private land, you are trespassing unless you ask permission. If the fruit is on public land, you have two considerations. One is the plant or tree. In the old days, people often plucked fruit by breaking off a bough and carrying it away. In Robert Browning's poem "The Last Duchess" there is a line. "The bough of cherries some officious fool broke in the orchard for her..."

Today we know cherries are too precious to break off boughs, even wild cherries.

Second, we consider other users of wild fruit — both human and animal — and we leave a share of them.

The ten basic rules for using wild food (Chapter II) apply as much to fruit as to greens and roots. You want to enjoy the fruit but you do not want to get poisoned.

Serviceberry

Amelanchier alnifolia

Serviceberry is one of the first wild fruits of the season. It may not always ripen in June as one common name, Juneberry, implies, but it is ripe by July.

You can spot the bushes in spring by their feathery racemes of fragrant white flowers. Serviceberry is the most common white-flowered bush of the early spring season in many areas. It blooms before chokecherry.

The bushes grow from three to 25 feet tall. The leaves turn red, orange and yellow in fall. The bright fall color and the pretty spring blooms make the shrub attractive enough to be planted in gardens.

The berries, about the size of a blueberry, are reddish-purple when ripe. Later in the season, they turn dark purple.

This fruit was an important food for the Indians and was used both fresh and dried. It was an ingredient of the famous pemmican, which was a concentrated trail food made of lean dried meat, dried fruit and rendered fat. Mince meat pie could be called a modern version of pemmican.

Saskatoon was the name given to serviceberries by the early settlers who simplified the Indian name mis-sask-qua-too-min. There is a city in Saskatchewan, Canada, named Saskatoon.

The white settlers quickly learned to appreciate serviceberry. They did not have vitamin pills and year-round fresh fruit and vegetables as we do, so the first fruits of the season were a welcome addition to their diet.

Serviceberry, also called sarviceberry and shadberry, has a sweet but bland taste. In a way, this is good. It is one of the few wild fruits you can eat to your heart's content without getting sick.

You can make pie or pudding or fruit sauce, but don't expect serviceberry to produce your favorite dessert. The berries don't cook apart and they have large seeds. Also, there is no acid so there is no tang. You have to add lemon juice, rhubarb, apple or wild plum. There are several varieties of serviceberry and even in the same patch, some bushes have a better quality berry than others.

You can make jam or jelly by adding acid and pectin, in addition to sugar, in order to get a proper jell.

Jelly is the better product because the jam is seedy unless you pass the cooked fruit through a sieve. I have found that picking the berries early in the season, as soon as they are barely ripe, gives the best fruit. As the berries stay on the bush, they get sweeter but the seeds grow larger.

You can also can the fruit or use it to make wine.

The Indians dried the fruit for winter use. Some tribes steam-cooked the berries before drying them. The fruit was put in a tub made of spruce bark and heated with layers of red-hot stones. According to a traveling journalist of the day, the bark method of cooking produced a better-tasting fruit than cooking in a brass or copper kettle.

After being dried, the fruit was pounded into cakes which could be kept for years. The cakes weighed 10 to 15 pounds. Pieces were broken off and soaked in water then added to soup or stew.

The best use I make of serviceberry is to eat it straight from the bush. I prefer to save my jars and freezer space for blueberries and applesauce. Also, I like to think of the birds and bears feasting on this early fruit.

Wild Strawberry

Fragaria virginiana

Wild strawberry vies with the blueberry and huckleberry in the contest for the tastiest wild fruit. Izaak Walton used the quotation "Doubtless God could have made a better berry but doubtless He never did" to state his case.

Most of us cannot judge because we cannot find wild strawberries. Birds, bears, chipmunks and mice beat us to the patches.

We have to content ourself with the cultivated strawberry and that, according to the experts, is a pale imitation as far as sweetness and flavor go.

Wild strawberries, of course, would never do for a mass market. They are too small and too perishable.

The French are credited with developing the cultivated strawberry. The wild berry was known and enjoyed as far back as ancient Rome.

The wild strawberry hides its fruit. You have to look under the leaves to find it, and it's very small. But once in a while, you find enough to pick and then you are in for a rare treat.

The wild plant grows close to the ground and puts out runners just as the cultivated plant does. The blossoms have five white petals. The leaves are divided into three leaflets.

There are two main species of wild strawberries, divided into several varieties. Some grow in meadows, some in open woods, often along roads that go through the woods.

The fruit is ripe in early summer. Any recipe for cultivated strawberries will do for the wild fruit, with first choice going to shortcake.

Uncooked freezer jam is good because it preserves the aroma of the wild berry. The genus name *Fragaria* means fragrance. We forget this because the cultivated berries have lost some of that delectable fragrance. Freezer jam uses powdered commercial pectin. The recipe is included in the package.

If you can't find fruit, you can pick the leaves for tea and console yourself with the fact that the leaves are full of vitamin C. In fact, an oldtime remedy for early spring let-down was tea made from freshly picked wild strawberry leaves, sometimes picked even from under snow. Vitamin C is soluble in water so the tea would act like a vitamin pill.

We know now that some of the illnesses that often appeared in late winter and early spring were due to a lack of vitamin C. There was no daily orange juice in those days.

You can make strawberry leaf tea out of freshly picked leaves or out of thoroughly dry ones but it is recommended not to use ones that have sat around and wilted. A toxin develops in the wilted leaves but it is destroyed by complete drying.

Strawberry leaf tea is used by some people as a cure for diarrhea.

One old name for strawberry fruit is earth mulberry. Another name — and some people say this is the origin of strawberry — is strewberry coming from strewn berry and referring to the way the berries are scattered or strewn among the leaves.

Currants and Gooseberries

Ribes (many species)

Golden Currant *(Ribes aureum)*

Mountain Gooseberry *(Ribes montigenum)*

There are so many species of wild currants and gooseberries that you will find it very hard to tell them apart. None are poisonous but some are distinctly inedible.

Botanists classify the *Ribes* species with spines as gooseberries and the *Ribes* without spines as currants. There are some species on the borderline, such as gooseberry currant and prickly currant.

The leaves of the currants and gooseberries are lobed like those of the maple but, of course, they are very small. The leaves are deciduous, meaning they turn color in autumn and fall off the bushes.

The flowers of the different *Ribes* vary in color from white to pink to yellow. The fruit varies in color also: red, black, orange, yellow or greenish. It can be smooth, or covered with hairs. It can have prickles or it can be sticky. One species has black berries that are almost dry.

The fruit can be used raw or cooked. Some species taste good, some are sour, some are bitter. Older fruit can be wormy.

You can make jelly out of several of the species: golden currant *(Ribes aureum)*, whitestem gooseberry *(R. inerme)*, black currant *(R. americanum)*, sticky currant *(R. viscosissimum)*, mountain gooseberry *(R. montigenum)*, and others.

Golden currant is a shrub three to eight feet tall. The name comes from the tubular, bright yellow flowers. The odor of the flowers is fragrant in a spicy way, hence another common name for the plant — clove bush.

This shrub is attractive enough to be planted in gardens. The fruits can be yellow, red, orange or black and they are large compared to other currants. To me, they look like the yellow-green gooseberries I remember from back east but the golden currant bush doesn't have spines.

Whitestem gooseberry *(Ribes inerme)* grows about four feet tall, with prickly stems and purple-black berries. Mountain gooseberry *(R. montigenum)* has sharp spines and reddish fruit. It is also called alpine prickly currant. It grows in subalpine to alpine areas.

Currants and gooseberries have their own pectin, especially if you pick the fruit before it is fully ripe, so you will not have to use commercial pectin. You might want to add apple juice for flavor. If you want to try jam, you could experiment. Try some pure currant or gooseberry, some mixed with rhubarb, some mixed with apple.

The Indians used currants and gooseberries in pemmican.

The *Ribes* shrubs bloom in spring and the fruit ripens, depending on the species and the altitude, any time from early summer to fall.

Red Raspberry

Rubus idaeus

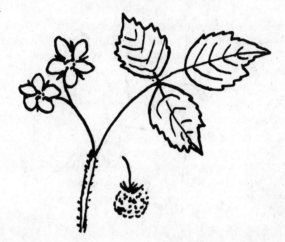

The wild red raspberry is the ancestor of our cultivated varieties. Through selective breeding, the cultivated canes give much more fruit and of a much larger size.

Wild red raspberry *(Rubus idaeus)* is native to North America and Eurasia. There are two varieties.

The stalks, called canes, grow from two to five feet tall and have prickles. They grow in woods and on open rocky slopes.

The wild fruit is small. Sometimes it hardly looks like a raspberry at all. In clearings, where the plants get sun, the fruit is larger. A good place to find wild red raspberry is in areas where a forest fire has been.

The leaves are compound with generally three leaflets, notched around the edges. The leaves are soft. One variety has down on the under surface. The five-petaled flowers are white and bloom in June and July.

Some people make tea from the leaves. Use either fresh from the canes or well dried. Do not use wilted leaves. It is recommended to use this tea sparingly as it is known to be a home remedy, one use being to cure diarrhea.

The fruit is ripe in midsummer and is excellent for eating fresh or to make jam. It can also be frozen or canned.

The *Rubus* genus contains many other edible fruits. Thimbleberry is *Rubus parviflorus* Blackcap or black raspberry is *R. occidentalis* or *R. leucodermis*. Blackberry is *R. ursinus*.

There are other lesser known *Rubus* fruits such as salmonberry, wineberry and nagoonberry.

Thimbleberry

Rubus parviflorus

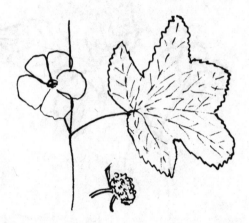

Thimbleberry is a relative of the raspberry and blackberry. All these plants are in the *Rubus* genus of the rose family.

Thimbleberry is *Rubus parviflorus* and it is a shrub without prickles. The wild red raspberry and the blackberry have prickles on the stems.

Thimbleberry is a showy plant. It forms a dense underbrush two to six feet high in open woods and at the edge of mountain roads. The leaves are large — up to eight inches across — coarse and lobed like a maple leaf. The white flowers are shaped like a wild rose.

The fruit looks like a pale red, flattened raspberry. It is edible but don't expect it to compare with the raspberry. The thimbleberry fruit gets mushy when ripe. Some people find the taste good — sweet yet tart. Other people say the fruit is insipid. It can be eaten raw or made into preserves.

The flowers are found in late spring and early summer. The fruit is ripe in late summer.

The plant grows from Alaska south to New Mexico.

The word salmonberry is sometimes used interchangeably with thimbleberry but the plant most botanists prefer to call salmonberry is another *Rubus* – *R. spectabilis,* which is found from Alaska south to northern California. It has red flowers and pinkish-yellow fruit.

The name salmonberry is generally believed to come from the use the northwest Indians made of the fruit. They ate the berries along with partially dried salmon eggs. Probably thimbleberry was used in the same way and therefore acquired the same name.

Oldtimers made tea by boiling thimbleberry leaves. Today we advocate steeping only, which means to pour boiling hot water on the leaves and let them sit about five minutes.

Blueberry

Thin-leaved Blueberry
(Vaccinium membranaceum)

The blueberry needs no introduction. It is the favorite fruit in many areas. In a good year, you can pick a gallon in an hour. Then you are king of the kitchen with pies, cobblers, tarts, pancakes, muffins, fruit dumplings. Any fruit dish becomes a delicacy when made with blueberries.

There is some confusion between the names blueberry and huckleberry. Botanically the true huckleberry is in the *Gaylusaccia* genus. Many of the berries called huckleberry are botanically in the *Vaccinium* genus and that is the blueberry group.

But it does not matter. Common names belong to the people who use them. If you want to call a certain berry huckleberry and your neighbor wishes to call it a blueberry, don't get excited. It is done everywhere.

For instance, the blueberry *Vaccinium membranaceum,* which has fruit almost a half-inch in diameter, is called by at least four common names: big whortleberry, black huckleberry, tall bilberry and thin-leaved blueberry.

This proliferation of common names is the reason why botanists must use the Latin name. Anywhere in the world, in any language, *Vaccinium membranaceum* is *Vaccinium membranaceum.*

Most people do not try to tell one species of blueberry from another.

103

The one that is quite different is grouseberry, or grouse whortleberry, which is *V. scorparium* and has slender broomlike branches only a foot high and tiny bright red berries. The plant and the berries seem just the right size for grouse so it is aptly named.

The flowers of the blueberry are tiny urns, pink or white. They bloom in early summer. The fruit is ripe in midsummer.

The leaves are alternate on the bushes and are deciduous, meaning they drop off in the fall.

The shape of the berry varies from round to oval and the color varies from black to blue to purple to red. Some species have a dusky blue covering called bloom. The fruit of all the species is deep purple when cooked and it all tastes delicious.

We who live in the Rockies call our *Vaccinium* berries huckleberries. We know they are in the same genus as the blueberries that are sold in the market but we also know they have a much richer taste than the blueberries sold in the market and they deserve a distinctive name. If you like, we'll settle for Rocky Mountain huckleberries.

Anyway, they are a marvelous fruit with a marvelous taste, plus a fragrance so distinctive people often say they are led to patches by their nose.

Some years there are so many berries, people pick them to sell commercially. Other years the crop is so scarce homemakers mix their wild berries half and half with store blueberries. The rich taste of the wild berry predominates, so you hardly notice the store berries. The wild berry taste is both sweet and tart, in exactly the right proportions.

If you want to make the best use of a small amount of wild berries you can put them in pancakes or muffins. If you have more, you can make a pie or cobbler. When you have a surplus, you can preserve them for winter by canning, freezing, making jelly and jam, or drying.

The Indians dried the berries and used them in pemmican, in soups, and as a sauce for meat.

The fruit does not have enough pectin to make jelly or jam. You have to use commercial pectin or a concentrated apple juice from tart, slightly underripe apples.

The fruit is one of the major food sources of bears. They travel many miles searching for the berries. They certainly follow their nose.

Cranberry

Vaccinium macrocarpon

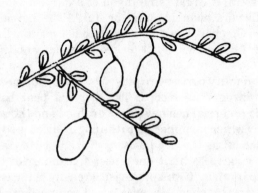

If you eat a cranberry raw, without sugar, there is no magic in it at all. It is so sour you wonder how anyone ever discovered its marvelous flavor. The scientific name for the small wild cranberry is *oxycoccus,* meaning "sour berry" and the name certainly fits.

But even the pre-Puritan-era Indians enjoyed cranberry sauce with their roasted wild turkey. The Indians discovered cranberry sauce. They used honey or maple sugar as a sweetener.

Today most of our cranberries are grown commercially. Two-thirds of the crop is raised in Massachusetts and the rest in New Jersey, Wisconsin, Oregon and Washington. The commercial variety is *Vaccinium macrocarpon,* which is one of the two original wild species, the larger one.

Perhaps you recognize the genus name, *Vaccinium.* It is the genus name of blueberry. The blueberry and cranberry are relatives, since they are both in the heath family.

If you went to a cranberry bog to see the berries growing, you would find a mass of creeping evergreen plants, almost reminding you of kinnikinnick, but the cranberry stalks are stouter and grow higher.

The commercial cranberry, also called large, American or bog cranberry, is native to northern U. S. and Canada, growing in acid bogs.

V. oxycoccus has smaller berries and is native south to the Carolinas and west to Wisconsin. Sweden has a cranberry called lingonberry which grows on mountains and sometimes has the common name of mountain cranberry or cowberry. This berry became quite famous during one of the World Fairs held in New York. Swedish lingonberry waffles were the thing to try. The idea was sort of a waffle sandwich with fruit and cream in the center.

The name cranberry was originally craneberry and came from the shape of the flower and bud. The bud is oval and as it hangs at the end of an inch-long stem, it could remind you of a crane's head and neck.

The pink flowers open in June or July. The berries are ripe in September and October. The color varies from a very dark red to mottled red and white. The berries, if not picked, often stay on the plants until spring.

The highest quality berries are picked by hand, but most of the crop is harvested by large rake scoops. The original peat bogs which are prepared for commercial use have been drained and the water collected into a reservoir which is connected to the bog by ditches so the bog can be flooded or dried off as the need arises.

One does not have to limit one's use of cranberries to the holiday turkey accompaniment. Cranberries jell so easily children can have fun making their first batch of jelly or jam. All you need are berries, sugar and water.

You can also make raw cranberry relish, chiffon pie, cranberry whip or a sherbert. A two-crust cranberry pie is sometimes called "mock cherry" because the taste is so similar.

Raw cranberries keep well. They are so hardy that, back in the days of sailing ships, wild cranberries were shipped from America to Europe and they kept during all that time. The berries were put in barrels and covered with water.

Both the leaves and berries have medicinal value. The leaves are useful in kidney disorders. They have a diuretic property. The berries are said to be good for removing blood toxins and are effective in proper liver function.

If there is anything we need after the usual heaped-high Thanksgiving feast, it is a good digestive aid. So bring on the cranberry, whether bought in the market or picked in the wild.

Fairy-bell

Wartberry Fairy-bell *(Disporum trachycarpum)*

Fairy-bell is a dainty flower found in moist woods of the type a poet would describe as "a sylvan dell where fairies dwell."

The plant grows one to two feet tall and is branched and leafy, with most of the leaves at the top. The flowers are fragile cream-colored or greenish-white bells hanging from the tips of the branches but not easy to see because they are hidden under the leaves. The flower petals flare outward. Blooming season is April through June.

The flowers turn into red berries so the plant is just as pretty in late summer as in spring. The berries are redish-orange or yellow and have a rough, velvety-textured, warty surface: hence the name wartberry fairy-bell.

This species is *Disporum trachycarpum.* The other fairy-bell of the Rockies is *D. hookeri,* variety *oreganum,* which is called Hooker or Oregon fairybell. It has a berry also red or yellow in color but not warty and more oval in shape.

The berries of both species are edible and are rather sweet, but the supply is so small books on edible plants usually do not mention them. Rodents and birds put the berries to good use.

Fairy-bell could be confused with twisted-stalk and solomon-plume. All these plants grow in shady woods and have parallel-veined leaves. But twisted-stalk has a definite kink or twist in the flower stem and solomon-plume does not branch.

Mandarin is a common name sometimes applied to fairy-bell.

Twisted-stalk

Streptopus amplexifolius

Twisted-stalk is a lush leafy plant of moist woods and streambanks. It grows in branched form two to four feet tall with ovate leaves alternating on the stalk. The leaves have parallel veins and look almost pleated.

The flowers are white or greenish-white bells with back-curving petals.

You could easily miss the flowers because they hang from the axils of the leaves and are often hidden. There is generally only one flower in each axil.

The flower stem has a distinct kink or twist in it and that is a distinguishing characteristic. The scientific name, *Streptopus amplexifolius,* describes the plant exactly: *Streptopus* coming from two Greek works meaning twisted and foot; and *amplexifolius* meaning clasping-leaved.

The kink in the flower stem is a way to tell twisted-stalk from fairy-bell. The two plants are very similar, both having whitish flowers hanging under the leaves, both growing in wet woods, both flowering late spring to early summer.

The flowers of twisted-stalk turn into dark red or orange berries which are smooth and clear — as contrasted with the velvety berries of fairy-bell. The berries are edible and were used by the Indians. Grouse are fond of them.

The young spring shoots can be eaten but it is not easy to identify the plant in that stage.

Cucumber-root or wild cucumber are common names given to

twisted-stalk because the new shoots when used raw, as in a salad, have a cucumber-like flavor.

Other common names are white mandarin, liverberry and scootberry. The latter name comes from the laxative effect of the berry and warns us against overindulgence.

Solomon-plume

Smilacina racemosa

Solomon-plume is often called false solomon-seal. The plant has an unbranched stem with large leaves and a terminal cluster of small creamy-white flowers. It grows two to three feet tall.

The scientific name is *Smilacina racemosa*.

The reason *Smilacina* is called false solomon-seal is that in the east, where true solomon-seal is found, the two plants often grow side by side and the leaf and stalk structure is quite similar.

However, true solomon-seal is a different genus. It would be best all around if *Smilacina racemosa* were called solomon-plume and forget the seal part.

The flower cluster is like a plume so solomon-plume is quite suitable.

Other common names are wild spikenard and treacleberry.

The plume of *Smilacina racemosa* develops into round juicy speckled berries. The color is red with purple flecks.

These berries are edible, either raw or cooked. They are rather bittersweet and can act as a laxative, so you may prefer to leave them for the ruffed grouse.

The Indians used them. They also used the thick rootstocks. They soaked the rootstocks in lye to get rid of the bitter taste. Then they parboiled them to get rid of the lye.

The young tender shoots can be used as a potherb or substitute for asparagus.

There are two species of *Smilacina* in the Rockies. *S. stellata* is smaller and the flowers are sparser in the cluster. A common name for *S. stellata* is wild lily-of-the-valley. Another name is starry solomon-plume. The tiny flowers look like six-pointed stars.

The berries of *S. stellata* are edible to the extent of the *S. racemosa* berries.

If experimenting, be sure you do not confuse *Smilacina* berries with the poisonous baneberry. Baneberry fruit can be red or white.

Smilacina blooms from May through July. It is found in woods, thickets and open meadows.

Sumac

Smooth Sumac *(Rhus glabra)*

Next summer try pink lemonade made from the fruit of the smooth sumac.

Sumac grows wild and is also an ornamental for gardens and parks. It is a shrub or small tree with fern-like leaves which turn brilliant red in the fall and compact velvety clusters of dark red berries.

To make the lemonade, just break off the clusters of berries, immerse in water, strain the juice, sweeten and drink.

Some people say to use hot water, others prefer cold because there is

tannin in the berries and hot water will extract more of this substance. In fact, a concentrated infusion of sumac berries is an astringent gargle good for sore throat.

You have to strain the juice through several thicknesses of cloth or fine hairs will be in the lemonade.

The secret of good sumac lemonade is to drink it right after making it. The flavor changes very rapidly.

Sumac berries are acid, so if you are making elderberry jelly, you can substitute sumac fruit juice for the lemon juice most recipes require.

Smooth or western sumac, *Rhus glabra,* grows two to eight feet tall. The tall sumac often planted in parks is staghorn sumac, *Rhus typhina,* which can grow 10 to 20 feet tall and is native to eastern U.S.A.

The name staghorn comes from the fact that the young branches are covered with down and look like a deer's antlers "in the velvet." Smooth sumac does not have this velvet.

Both smooth and staghorn sumac have edible berries, the staghorn fruit being more acid. In fact, sometimes it is called vinegar tree.

Indians gathered the fruit of both and dried them for winter use. A hot "lemonade" sweetened with maple syrup was a winter drink of eastern Indians.

Sumac fruit stays on the bushes throughout winter and is eaten by birds.

The leaves of western sumac were sometimes added to the tobacco of the Indians.

Squawbush is another sumac, *Rhus trilobata,* and its berries are also good for a beverage.

There are some poisonous relatives of the sumac — poison ivy and poison sumac — but the poisonous species have white berries, so if you stick to only red-berried sumacs, you will be all right.

Ground-cherry

Long-leaved Ground-cherry *(Physalis longifolia)*

Ground-cherry is not a cherry, but rather a relative of the tomato. One species is grown in gardens and called Chinese lantern plant. It has very attractive orange seed husks that look exactly like tiny replicas of Chinese lanterns, hence the name.

Some species of ground-cherry are edible. The fruit is inside the papery husks and is rather like a miniature tomato or pitless cherry.

As a wildflower, the ground-cherries are coarse plants growing from six to 25 inches tall, along roadsides, in wasteland and in cultivated fields.

Long-leaved ground-cherry, *Physalis longifolia,* is a perennial with two varieties, one more common in the east and the other more common in the west.

This ground-cherry has bell-shaped yellow flowers turning purple in the center. The leaves are roughly egg-shaped or triangular.

Ground-cherry fruit is about one-half inch in diameter. The color varies, depending on the species, from yellow to red to brown.

If you are going to eat the fruit, be sure it is ripe. The unripe fruit — and the foliage also — has toxic properties. You can eat the fruit raw, as a dessert or sliced into a salad like tomatoes. Cooked, the fruit makes a good pie or jam.

There are several edible species. The old-time Mesa Verde Indians made wide use of the fruit. They ate it raw, or mixed into a relish along with onions and chili, or dried and ground up for meal.

Another common name for ground-cherry is bladder-cherry. The papery husk does look like an inflated bladder and that is the origin of the scientific name *physalis*. It comes from the Greek for bladder.

Prickly Pear

Opuntia polyacantha

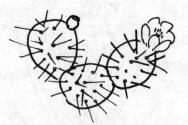

Prickly pear is not a pear. It is a cactus. It has edible parts but the entire plant, even the fruit, is covered with sharp spines. You need gloves to handle it.

One of the most common species is *Opuntia polyacantha* which is made up of pads or joints, three to six inches long, forming low-growing clumps.

The joints are really stems, not leaves, but they take the place of leaves. The joints store moisture, thus enabling the plant to withstand droughts.

The joints can be eaten raw or cooked but you are faced with the job of removing the needle-like spines. You could slice them off with a knife or burn them off. Ranchers in the southwest have sometimes used cacti for emergency cattle feed after burning off the spines.

The showy yellow flowers come out on the edges of the joints and are followed by small fruits that look like little knobs.

The fruit can be eaten raw or cooked but you have to remove the barbs. If you have leather gloves you can rub the barbs off.

Some of the *Opuntia* species, especially those in Mexico, have fruit large enough to be worth the trouble of harvesting and selling in the market. Tourists find it under the name "tuna."

The part eaten is the pulp between the mass of seeds in the center and the tough outer skin. It is sweet and tasty.

The indians preserved the fruit by drying it in the sun. You hear the name Indian fig sometimes used for the fruit.

The color can vary from yellow-green to purple to red.

Yucca

Spanish Bayonet *(Yucca glauca)*

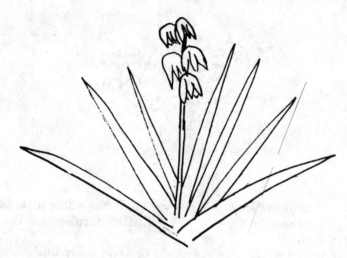

Yucca is a plant that grows in dry sandy soil and looks as if it should be related to the cacti but actually it is in the lily family. There are many species and several are edible.

Spanish bayonet, *Yucca glauca,* is one of the common edible yuccas. If you try to handle the leaves you will know why the plant has the name bayonet. The leaves are stiff and as sharp-pointed as a dagger.

The flowering stalk, which comes up in the middle of the clump of leaves, can be five feet tall. The large greenish-white or creamy-white flowers hang like bells. The flowers are almost closed in daytime but at night they open and are pollinated by the white yucca moth.

The fruit of *Y. glauca,* when ripe, is a dry pod. The Indians used it while it was green. They baked it in the ashes or dried it in the sun. It has a bitter taste and would not be considered a delicacy by most people.

114

The flowers can be eaten raw or cooked. The heart of the young flowering stalk can be eaten boiled or roasted. It is fibrous but in an emergency would provide sustenance.

There are some yucca species that have fleshy fruit. The Indians split open this fruit and used the pulp. The large black seeds were also used, either roasted or ground into meal.

Yucca in any form is not a food you would prize. The common names soapwell and soapweed tell you that the plants contain saponin. The roots of many species will lather in water. The Indians and early settlers made use of this detergent quality to wash their clothes and hair.

It is advised not to eat any parts of the yucca plants to excess. They can act as a laxative.

Yucca leaves have fibers that can be separated out and used to make twine and rope.

The eastern species with the name *Y. filamentosa* is very similar to *Y. glauca* and is also called Spanish bayonet.

Agave, or century plant, looks much like yucca and can be used in almost the same way. The sap, when fermented, makes the alcoholic drink tequila, sometimes called mescal.

Agave can be laxative, like yucca.

Bunchberry

Cornus canadensis

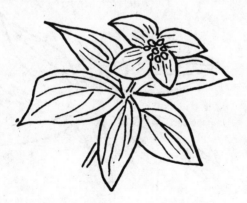

Bunchberry is a dogwood, even though it is only inches high and looks like a ground cover.

As is true of all dogwoods, what you think is a four-petaled white flower are really four bracts (modified leaves) surrounding a small cluster of true flowers.

The flowers of the bunchberry turn into a bunch of coral-red berries — hence the name bunchberry.

The plant grows in deep woods, preferring moist spongy soil. It spreads by underground runners, thus producing drifts of greenery.

The flowers are seen in late spring and early summer. The red berries can be found from August into fall, or until they are eaten by birds. Pigeon berry and chicken berry are names that denote the birds' liking for the fruit.

The berries are edible. They are not especially tasty but they are used for food in many parts of the world. The name puddingberry shows one of the uses that has been made of the fruit.

The Eskimos preserve the fruit for winter use. It can be eaten raw or cooked.

Bunchberry is sometimes called dwarf cornel, the cornel being a general term given to members of the *Cornus* or dogwood genus. Bunchberry is *Cornus canadensis,* Canadian dogwood.

It is native to northern North America and Asia.

The roots and bark have been used as a cold remedy. The bark can be a laxative.

In old Scotland, the plant had a reputation as the "plant of gluttony" because it was supposed to increase the appetite.

Red-osier Dogwood

Cornus stolonifera

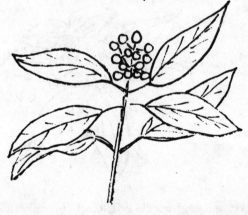

Red-osier dogwood does not look much like the 40-foot trees of the eastern flowering dogwood *(Cornus florida)* and the Pacific dogwood *(Cornus nuttallii).* These dogwoods have saucer-shaped flowers as big as a magnolia.

Red-osier dogwood grows only 15 feet high at its tallest but it is a handsome shrub. You find it in gardens and parks as well as in the wild. The red stems are one of the attractive features. In fact, red-stemmed dogwood is one of the other names for this plant. The French Canadians called it *bois rouge* meaning red forest or woods.

In May or June the opposite green leaves appear and soon after come the flat-topped clusters of flowers. The flowers are four-parted, and like all dogwoods, the showiest parts are not petals, but bracts. The flowers are in the center of the four bracts and are almost invisible. The bracts are white and for all general purposes look like four white petals.

Red-osier dogwood grows in moist soil in both flat land and mountains.

The inner bark was used in the old days for tobacco, either alone or mixed with true tobacco. The bark was dried in the sun or over the fire and was then rubbed between the hands and broken into small pieces.

The Indians ate the white berry. We would find it bitter and unappealing but we have so many fruits to choose from today. The Indians had to make do with what few berries they could find and then dry for the winter. Have you noticed, even today in our modern era, if you have been out camping or backpacking for a longer period of time than your fruit lasts, how eagerly you look for a stray huckleberry or wild currant?

If there aren't any of these berries left, you will even eat the insipid thimbleberry or the very sour Oregon-grape.

Meat and potatoes or fish and crackers fill you up and you can take a vitamin pill but you crave fruit. So the Indians gathered everything they could in the line of berries, even the bitter ones, and saved them to vary the winter diet.

Since we do not need the berries of red-osier dogwood, we will leave them for the birds and animals and we will content ourselves with admiring the rose-red fall foliage.

Elderberry

Blue Elderberry *(Sambucus cerulea)*

Elderberry pie does not compare with apple or huckleberry but for some people, it is a fall ritual — the leaves turn yellow, nights are frosty and for one Sunday dinner, mom makes an elderberry pie.

Before you dash out and start picking the fruit by the pailful, allow me to add a note of caution. Elderberry can make you sick.

117

Most people have no trouble with the fruit and some people eat the flowers too, but the plant does contain a toxic substance and you should be aware of the potential danger.

The toxic substance is an alkaloid and it can cause nausea, vomiting

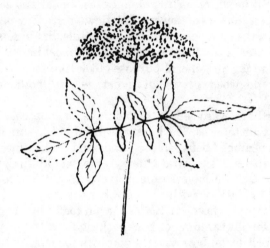

and diarrhea. The alkaloid is most potent in the green wood and the unripe fruit. Children have been made ill by cutting whistles and blowguns from the green wood and using them immediately. The Indians dried the wood before making their flutes and pipes. Elderberry wood has a pithy center that makes it a natural for whistles, pipes, etc.

Most people wait for the first frost to use the berries. By that time, they are generally completely ripe and also the frost causes an enzyme change in the fruit which produces a better taste.

Some people can eat raw fruit, others can eat only cooked fruit. A few people cannot tolerate any part of the elderberry.

I find the blue elderberry the most palatable. It is the one that grows quite tall — up to 15 feet — and has flat-topped clusters of pale powdery blue fruit.

There are several other species of elderberry. The red-berried elder (elder is another name for the plant) grows higher up in the mountains. I do not care for the fruit. It does not agree with me even when it is fully ripe. You can try it but I recommend trying only a little to start with. Don't make a pie and invite your friends over. Some of them will certainly get an upset stomach.

Even with the blue elderberry, I would recommend eating only a small amount until you know your reaction.

It is wise to learn to identify the different species by botanical name. The blue elderberry is *Sambucus cerulea*. Identify it by the flat-topped clusters of flowers and the pale blue fruit. The black elderberry is *Sambucus racemosa* but it has four varieties, some with black fruit, some purplish-black and some red. All of the four varieties have flowers in a pyramid shape and generally the bushes are smaller than *S. cerulea*. If you wish to try one of the four varieties, I would recommend the black-fruited *melanocarpa* variety. It is sometimes called black elder.

You can try eating the flowers, if you wish. I have eaten the flowers of *S. cerulea* in pancakes and in fritters. I picked fully ripe flowers and removed as much of the green stem as possible. Of course, for the fritters, you have to leave some stem to hold the flower cluster together.

Elderberry jelly can be made in several ways. You can use half apple or crabapple juice, or 100 per cent elderberry. There is no pectin in elderberry fruit so you have to add either concentrated apple juice or commercial pectin.

Wine can be made from either the fruit or the flowers, the latter being called "elder blow wine."

Elderberry fruit lacks acid, so the pie recipes sometimes call for lemon juice or apple or rhubarb.

When camping we use the fruit of the blue and the black elderberry as a breakfast drink. Just pick ripe fruit, cook in a large amount of water and add sugar to taste.

Elderberries can be dried and stored for winter use. Some people say the taste is improved by the drying process.

The eastern elderberry is *S. canadensis* which has purple-black berries that are as good as *S. cerulea*.

There is nutritive value in the elderberry: vitamin C, a little protein, some iron and quite a lot of potassium.

Cold remedies have been made from the fruit. One recipe is elderberry syrup mixed with honey. A more potent recipe is elderberry syrup mixed with brandy. This, of course, is a liqueur or cordial. Perhaps it is the elderberry that is the remedy and perhaps it is the alcohol.

The elderberry bush is easy to recognize. It is a large shrub, almost a tree in some species. The leaves are compound like a fern's and grow opposite on the stem.

The shrubs grow in moist meadows and along riverbanks and mountain streams.

Common Barberry

Berberis vulgaris

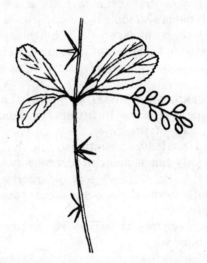

If you read in an oldtime recipe book how to make barberry jelly or barberry syrup, don't dash out to the garden and strip the little red football-shaped fruits from your hedge.

Likely you have the species called Japanese barberry *(Berberis thunbergii)* and you will find that the berries are dry and not at all satisfactory.

The barberry used in the recipe books is common barberry *(Berberis vulgaris)* which is also an import but it has become so well established it acts like a native.

The reason gardens in many areas have Japanese barberry is because common barberry is prohibited. It is a host of black-stem wheat rust. Japanese barberry does not harbor the disease.

Most recipes talking about barberries came from New England where farmers did not grow wheat. They could enjoy their barberries, or sourberries, as they called them. They made wine, preserves and jelly, and dried or pickled the berries.

A drink was made by adding lemon, mint and sugar to the extracted juice. This drink was known as long ago as the days of ancient Egypt. It was supposed to be good for fevers and jaundice.

An old copy of "New England Farmer" touted barberry jelly as the "only thing" to serve with venison. But we have many things to serve with venison. One has to remember when reading old recipe books that the good taste of some of those products depended on the scarcity of better ones.

Also, sometimes the method of preparation produced an exotic flavor that we do not get in our quick-cooking save-fuel methods. For instance, that venerable copy of "New England Farmer" said, in order to extract the juice from the barberries, you "heat the berries in a close-covered stone jar, without water, till the juice flows."

A New England hearth oven could do that perfectly but would we today want to spend that much time?

The publication also said, "Every thoroughbred housekeeper will put up barberry syrup when she learns its value for invalids' use."

We can enjoy reading about barberry jelly and syrup but we have many other fruits that are easier to work with, so we can leave the barberries on the bushes to be softened by the weather until birds use them as an emergency food supply.

You can tell if your hedge is Japanese barberry by looking at the leaves and spines. Common barberry has saw-toothed leaves, spines in groups of three and its berries in racemes.

Japanese barberry has smooth-edged leaves. The spines grow singly and the berries grow singly or in pairs.

Some barberry shrubs are evergreen. Japanese barberry and common barberry lose their leaves in the fall, after they have turned a brilliant red.

Oregon-grape

Berberis repens

Oregon-grape is not a grape — it is a barberry. It is in the same classification as the garden ornamental called Japanese barberry. Oregon-grape can also be grown in gardens, especially the upright kind which is a shrub two to four feet tall.

The common wild species in the Rockies is *Berberis repens,* or creeping Oregon-grape. It grows a foot high. In spring, it has bright yellow flowers and in fall, the leaves turn lovely colors — red and orange and bronze.

The powdery blue berries grow close to the ground in small culsters, the size of the berries being that of a small wild grape — hence the name Oregon-grape.

The taste is like wild grape too — very tart. Few people eat Oregon-grape berries raw.

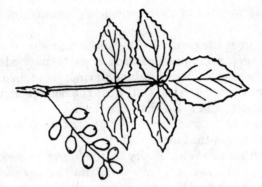

I make a fruit juice that is purple and rich. I think it compares well with store-bought grape juice. To make it, I boil ripe Oregon-grape fruit in water and strain it, then add sugar to taste. If the juice is very concentrated, I add water.

This same juice can be made into jelly. For jelly, I mix the Oregon-grape juice with apple or crabapple juice. This accomplishes two purposes: one, it dilutes the Oregon-grape tartness; two, it adds pectin. Some people make pure Oregon-grape jelly. They simply add sugar and boil until it is thick. I prefer half apple juice. Then I use very ripe Oregon-grape fruit and depend on apple or crabapple for the pectin which is needed to jell the jelly.

You could also use commercial pectin. The recipe for Concord grape jelly in the commercial pectin recipes will serve for Oregon-grape.

Oregon-grape is also called holly-grape. The name refers to the hollylike leaves. Note the spiny teeth. The leaves are evergreen in some areas, in others they turn color. You will notice, when you walk in the woods in winter, you can find both dark green leaves and bright red ones.

The yellow-wooded stems and roots have been used both as a source of dye and as a source of medicine — a bitter tonic.

The upright kind of Oregon-grape is the state flower of Oregon. Its fruit is exactly like that of the low creeping Oregon-grape and can be used in the same way.

Wild Grape

Riverbank Grape (*Vitis riparia*)

Wild grapes are smaller and more tart than cultivated grapes. They can be eaten as is but mostly they are used for jelly, grape juice and wine.

There are many species, some better-tasting than others.

The plants are vines or vining shrubs with hard-wooded stems. Tendrils on the stems enable the climbing species to reach as high as the tops of trees. The leaves are alternate and shaped rather like a maple leaf.

Cultivated grapes were developed from the wild species. The greenish-yellow flowers are not conspicuous but they are very fragrant. Bees make honey from the nectar and some people regard this honey as exceptionally good.

Riverbank grape, *Vitis riparia,* a native of eastern U.S., grows in both eastern and western regions. The fruit was important to the Indians and pioneers.

Grape leaves are used in many parts of the world in cooking. One dish is dolmas, stuffed grape leaves. The stuffing can be meat or a rice-meat-herb mixture. The young shoots have been used as a potherb.

Do not confuse wild grape with Virginia creeper, *Parthenocissus quinquefolia,* which is also a vine and has leaves and berries somewhat similar to some species of grape. Virginia creeper fruit is not edible.

Hawthorn

River Hawthorn *(Crataegus douglasii)*

Hawthorns are shrubs or small trees known for their stout thorns. They are sometimes called thornapple but that is not a good name to use when talking about edible wild plants because the same name is used for a poisonous plant. *Datura stramonium* is called thornapple and it has killed people. This is an example of the necessity for using scientific names for plants. Common names can be confusing.

The scientific name for river hawthorn, also called black haw or western black hawthorn, is *Crataegus douglasii*. It has black fruit rather similar in size, shape and color to serviceberry or huckleberry. Usual location is near rivers and streams.

Sometimes you see the Latin name *Crataegus rivularis* used for this same species. *Rivularis* refers to the location near running water.

River hawthorn grows in the form of a small tree, up to 25 feet. The small white spring-blooming flowers are five-petaled and fragrant. The tree has thorns strong enough to make a survival fishhook.

The leaves turn color in the fall, showing bright oranges and reds.

The fruit is edible but not very exciting. It contains rather large bony seeds called nutlets. Sometimes the fruit has enough pulp around the seeds to make it worth eating. Other times, it seems to be all seeds.

The Indians used the fruit fresh and dried. It was an ingredient of their pemmican. The early settlers made jam and jelly. A fruit sauce can be made by cooking the fruit (called haws) and then straining through a sieve.

I have made syrup which was very good — thick and good-tasting and of a pretty color. However, I don't like to use too much wild fruit just to make syrup or jelly. It seems to me I am taking fruit away from the bears and birds and then using only the essence. The wild animals use the whole fruit and they depend on it.

The fruit of river hawthorn stays on the branches well into winter and is a good survival food for wildlife.

The hawthorn species called red haw *(Crataegus columbiana)* has red fruit and longer, thinner spines. There are several eastern hawthorns with red fruit that is used for jelly.

Many hawthorn species are grown as ornamentals in gardens and parks.

The name black haw is used in the east for an entirely different shrub, a viburnum. It also has edible black fruit.

Wild Plum

Prunus americana

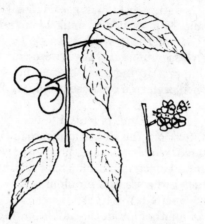

The common wild plum is *Prunus americana,* a native tree that grows throughout the United States but varies from area to area. In some places the trees are 10 to 15 feet tall, other places they are small shrubs. Sometimes the growth is in thickets. Some varieties have thorns, others don't.

The fruit also varies, one tree producing sweet fruit, others giving fruit so acid it can't be used unless cooked up with a great deal of sugar.

The color of the fruit can be red or yellow or a mottled purple. The size is about an inch across. The fruit is tough-skinned but excellent for jelly or jam.

Plums have their own pectin so commercial pectin is not needed. However, with the very sour types, you might prefer to make jelly using half plum juice and half that of another wild fruit that lacks acid, such as elderberries, chokecherries or serviceberries. The plums have the necessary acid and pectin to jell the combined juices.

Jam can be made in the same manner, combining plum with the pulp of fruits that are lacking in acid and pectin. I generally make jam instead of jelly because jam uses more of the fruit and I do not like to waste anything, even wild fruit. Jelly uses only the juice.

Jam also uses less sugar. Because it has the pulp that helps thicken the finished product, you can often use two-thirds cup sugar to one cup of fruit. Jelly needs a very exact amount of sugar or it will not set into jelly form. If you use commercial pectin, you will find that you are using more sugar than fruit — sometimes as much as six cups of sugar to four cups of fruit — for either jam or jelly. The advantage of the commercial pectin method is you have a foolproof method and you get a larger volume of finished jam or jelly. The disadvantage is you are eating a product that is 60 per cent sugar.

Using fruit that is naturally high in pectin like wild plums, underripe apples or crabapples allows you to make jam and jelly by the old-fashioned open-kettle method, which uses either an equal amount of sugar and fruit or a lesser amount of sugar: two-thirds or three-fourths.

Canning, freezing and drying are other methods of preserving fruit. Drying is the method preferred by those people who are trying to use as little sugar as possible.

The Indians dried many kinds of fruit, including wild plum. They cut the plums in half, took out the stones and spread the fruit in the sun.

We can do the same. We can also use the oven or we can make a simple drier that uses a small electric heater. There are many wild fruits that can be dried and then the storage problem is solved — no freezer, no sterilized jars with vacuum lids.

Fruit leather is another product that is gaining popularity. It is pureed fruit spread on plastic wrap on a cookie sheet and dried in the sun or in the oven or in a drier. A small amount of sugar can be added if it is necessary. Wild plum leather probably would need added sugar.

Plums are in the rose family, in the class of stone fruits such as cherry, peach and apricot.

The blossoms of wild plum are much like cherry — five-petaled, white or pinkish. They are fragrant and appear in spring before the leaves.

Chokecherry

Prunus virginiana

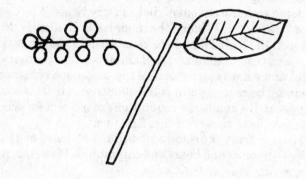

Chokecherry is a small wild cherry. The name describes the taste — astringent, puckery. It is not a fruit you would eat like raspberries or serviceberries. It is used mainly for syrup, jelly and wine.

Chokecherry is in the same genus as wild plum and the other stone fruits. Western chokecherry is *Prunus virginiana* variety *melanocarpa*. That means it is the same species as the eastern chokecherry but a different variety.

Chokecherry can be a shrub and it can be a tree. Botanically, a shrub does not have a single main stem. It branches close to the ground. A tree has a trunk. However, some plants grow in both forms. Chokecherry can be a small shrub only a few feet tall or it can be a twenty-foot tree.

It grows near streams both in valleys and on mountain slopes.

The white blossoms are in long racemes and flower just after serviceberry.

The fruit is red or black and is ripe in late August.

The Indians and early settlers made good use of the fruit. The settlers discarded the pits but the Indians used the whole fruit. They pounded it up, pits and all. Some tribes dried the fruit first, some pounded it up fresh then dried it. The dried fruit was used to flavor soups and stews, and it was a part of the important staple, pemmican.

The practice of using cherry pits is not recommended. It can be dangerous. Children have died from eating a large quantity of chokecherries without removing the pits.

The toxic substance is a cyanogenetic glycoside which produces hydrocyanic acid in the body. Some of the other stone fruits have this too.

The substance is rendered harmless by heat. That is why peach and apricot kernels can be added to cooked jam. The Indian method of drying

127

the pounded chokecherries in the sun would also change the toxic glycoside.

Chokecherry leaves and twigs also contain the poison. Livestock have died from eating the plant, especially in spring.

The Indians made a tea out of chokecherry twigs. White settlers had a recipe for "cherry tonic" using the inner bark. Evidently there is not so much poison in the bark and stems as there is in the leaves.

Also, we have to understand that there is a fine line between what is medicinal and what is poisonous. Many poisonous substances are used in medicine. The crucial point is the quantity. A little is a medicine — a lot is a poison. No doubt the reputations of old-time witch doctors and medicine men was poised on this fine line.

Chokecherry fruit is usually plentiful but most of it goes — and rightfully — to birds and bears and chipmunks. However, it can be used for wine, syrup, jelly or fruit soup.

To make syrup, boil the fruit until soft in enough water to cover, then strain through a jelly bag. Add about 1¾ cups of sugar to 1¼ cups of juice and boil hard for one minute. To preserve the syrup, can it in sterilized containers.

To make jelly, extract the juice in the same way, then follow a recipe for either commercial pectin jelly or old-fashioned boiled-down jelly.

I add apple juice to my chokecherry juice, so the jelly is half and half. I find that most wild fruits have a very pronounced flavor. A little goes a long way. The apple juice also adds the necessary acid and pectin. I use throw-away apples, those that are wormy or too small to be used otherwise. Crabapples can also be used. They are high in pectin, especially when underripe.

Fruit soup is a European idea. It is rather like a diluted, thickened fruit cup. It can be served hot or cold. You don't need a great deal of fruit, if you make fruit soup, because you add water and then thicken it with cornstarch, arrowroot, tapioca or ordinary flour. Flavor with cinnamon and orange or lemon peel.

This is the same principle as the Indians adding dried fruit to their various soups and stews.

Chokecherry wine is an old favorite. There are many recipes, some very simple, some very complicated.

Rose

Wild Woods Rose *(Rosa woodsii)*

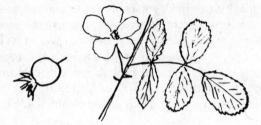

If you are driving along a highway and you see a person gathering the red seed pods of wild rose bushes, you might wonder what he is doing and why he is doing it.

He is making use of one of nature's richest sources of vitamin C. During World War II, tons of rose hips were collected in Britain and made into a syrup called National rose hip syrup. This syrup was doled out to children to take the place of citrus fruits which were not arriving. We ourselves can buy, in drug stores and health food shops, vitamin C tablets made from rose hips.

The rose hip is the fruit of the rose bush. It contains the seeds. Around the seeds is a red-orange pulp which is edible and which contains a phenomenal amount of vitamin C. Five or six hips provide your entire daily requirement. There is also vitamin A, calcium and iron.

Everyone knows the rose. It is both a wildflower and a cultivated flower. The cultivated roses, called hybrids, are developed from the wild ones.

The wild roses grow from three to 10 feet tall, usually have prickly branched stems and bloom with simple pink or pinkish white flowers May through July. The flowers have five petals. The leaves are alternate and divided into leaflets, usually five to seven. In some species the leaves turn brilliant red and orange in fall.

You find wild roses in valleys, along streams, and on hillsides if there is moist soil. The shrubs sometimes take over whole pastures.

The hips are ripe in August and September.

There is a great variation in the quality of rose hips. Some are all seeds, some have a large amount of pulp. None are poisonous, so just taste one here and there until you locate a patch with fleshy good-tasting fruit. I have found hips so good I have eaten them right off the bush with enjoyment.

But most of the hips are full of seeds and around the seeds are tiny hairs that tickle your throat. The best use of hips is for jam, jelly, a vitamin-rich syrup or a health tea.

There are many recipes for rose hip jam and jelly. If you want to preserve the most vitamin C, you could try uncooked freezer jam, using commercial powdered pectin. You have to remove the seeds and the hair around the seeds, which means each rose hip has to be cut in half and worked on. Unless you have in your yard a bush of Rugosa rose with its hips as big as a cherry, you will probably prefer cooking the hips and putting them through a sieve or ricer or food mill. Then you get a puree that looks like tomato soup and this puree can be made into jam, jelly or syrup.

I like rose hip and apple jam made from two cups of rose hip puree, two cups of apple puree and sugar to taste. If you are going to keep the jam on a shelf, you have to add quite a lot of sugar, almost an equal amount as fruit. If you are going to keep the jam in your refrigerator and eat it quickly, you can add less.

I have made good fruit leather out of the mixed rose hip and apple puree, adding very little sugar and drying it in my oven.

For jelly you strain the cooked, mashed rose hips through a jelly bag and extract a clear juice. If your rose hips seem to have a great deal of the fuzzy hair they might be better made into jelly than jam.

Crabapple juice can be added and that gives both needed acid and pectin.

To make syrup, you can strain the cooked mashed fruit through a bag, if you want a clear syrup, or through a sieve, if you want a thicker, honey-like syrup. I prefer the thicker syrup because I am using more of the fruit. I don't like to bring in a pailful of rose hips and take out only the essence and throw the rest away.

I make two extractions of juice from the cooked hips. After extracting one batch, I add water to the residue, cook it again and strain it again.

Rose hip syrup is preserved by canning, with or without sugar, in sterilized jars.

How much vitamin C you have in the syrup depends on many factors: one, how much there was in the original fruit; two, how long you boiled the fruit; three, what kind of cooking utensil you used. Vitamin C loss is greater in copper and aluminum kettles and less in glass or enamel.

The taste of rose hip syrup is not something to rave about but the product is nutritious. You can add it to many dishes. It gives a pretty salmon color to tapioca pudding.

Rose hip tea is made from the dried hips. Some people pulverize the hips immediately after drying and store them in powder form. I store mine whole and pulverize them as needed.

The tea is very mild in flavor. You can add cloves and cinnamon or a touch of honey.

There is vitamin E in the seeds but more research is needed. For instance, does our body absorb the vitamin E if we eat the seeds whole or do they have to be pulverized? Also, we should know whether there there is anything toxic in the seeds that might show up after prolonged use. Many wild foods have been used safely during their natural season but few studies have been made to show what happens if we tried to preserve the foods and use them on a regular basis.

Even though rose hip tea is made from dried hips, there is vitamin C in the tea. This is because the original hips have so much that even though some is lost in storage, some remains.

There is also carbohydrate in rose hips. If you were lost in the wilderness, rose hips could be a survival food. A group of Canadian explorers in the early 1800's lived on nothing but rose hips for almost a month.

Rose petals can be used in tea or in salads. Nip off the base because that is bitter.

Crabapple

Pyrus (many species)

Crabapple is both an ornamental tree and an edible fruit. The pink, white or red flowers are lovely in the spring and the red fruit in the fall is both lovely and useful.

Crabapple is in the *Pyrus* genus of the rose family. The *Pyrus* genus includes the common pear and the cultivated apple.

Some crabapples can be eaten right off the tree. Most are too sour.

But the marvelous thing about crabapples is they are full of pectin. And what is pectin? It is the ingredient that makes jelly jell. It is the ingredient you buy as a powder or syrup in stores and add to your fruit juice and sugar to make jelly.

You can extract the juice from crabapples and can it or freeze it to use with next year's strawberries and raspberries.

To get the best pectin yield and also the best flavor in the juice, don't use a pressure cooker to cook the crabapples. This goes for all fruit — not just crabapples. The very high heat of a pressure cooker destroys both flavor and pectin. If you destroy the pectin in your fruit, you have to add commercial pectin. You get more juice out of the fruit by using a pressure cooker but it's not as good quality.

Use slightly underripe crabapples and do not remove the skins or cores. Barely cover with water and simmer for 20 minutes or until soft, then strain through a jelly bag. I have used various non-commercial jelly bags, including gauze curtains, pillow cases and old flannel pajamas.

Crabapples also make good apple butter. Use the same recipe as for ordinary apples, either the open kettle method or the oven method. You can try out various kinds of crabapples for flavor before you make a big batch of butter. Your neighbor may have a better tasting variety than yours. There are dozens of species, some native, some imports.

Making fruit leather is almost the same process as making apple butter. You spread the sweetened mixture on thin plastic wrap on a cookie sheet and put it in the oven at very low heat until it dries into leather. Roll the leather in wax paper and cut into strips with scissors. This is a handy food for backpackers.

Hopa ornamental crab is the species of crabapple generally used for spiced or pickled crabapple because it is so pretty — bright red on the outside and pinkish-red on the inside. The recipe calls for sugar, vinegar, water, cinnamon, cloves and — if you feel like being extravagant — a sliced lemon.

The only native apple in America is the crabapple. Ordinary apples were brought from Europe by the early colonists. So-called "wild apples" are the ordinary apples escaped from cultivation. Birds and animals — and man — eat the fruit and spread the seeds.

If you have no apples or crabapples in your garden, you might politely ask a neighbor if you can make an exchange of labor for fruit. Offer to pick up all the fruit on the ground in return for a pailful to take home.

Mountain-ash

Sorbus scopulina

Mountain-ash has such lovely clumps of red berries a person feels he should do something with them. The old-time Indians ate them fresh and dried. The early white settlers made preserves and jelly.

I have tried the berries fresh and I have tried them cooked with sugar. I cannot recommend them at all. Raw, they are terribly bitter and also acid. Cooked with sugar, they are not acid but they are still bitter.

There might be some species that taste better than others. There are three species growing wild in the Rockies and there are species used as ornamental trees that come from eastern United States and Europe.

Mountain-ash is not an ash. The true ash tree is in the olive family. Mountain-ash is in the family of the rose and apple and hawthorn. But the leaves do have a resemblance to true ash leaves, hence the name.

Mountain-ash can be a shrub or a tree. The native Rocky Mountain species are shrubs, three to 15 feet tall. The eastern *Sorbus americana* is a tree growing to 30 feet.

The European mountain-ash is the rowan tree that is part of song and story of European literature. Ladies of the 18th and 19th centures sang: "We meet nae mair aneath the rowan tree." The rowan was also venerated by the Druids. In some parts, it was known as the "witchen" because it was supposed to ward off witches. An old ballad goes, "witches have no power where thrives the Rowan-tree wood..."

That tree, also called quickbeam, is tall, growing up to 60 feet.

The rowan seems to have berries that are more tasty than our native species, or maybe in the days when people really used the fruit, the larder was rather bare.

Books say, in times of scarcity, the berries were dried and ground into a meal and used as a substitute for bread. The authors admit the berries were sour and bitter, and the word for the meal was only "palatable," which is not really high praise.

We have to thank our supermarkets, refrigeration and canneries that we can have almost any fruit at any time. But who knows what will come in the future? There have been many eras when mankind lived on roots and berries.

In the mountains the native mountain-ash shrubs are part of the wildlife ecosystem. Moose browse the twigs and branches in the winter. The fruit is food for the bears before they hibernate and it is food for grouse all winter.

So let us not regret the sour and bitter taste. If we ate the berries, what would the wildlife have?

Buffaloberry

Silver Buffaloberry *(Shepherdia argentea)*

Buffaloberry used to take the place of cranberry sauce. It could also be made into pies. Today the berry is not important but people do make jelly of it.

It is found widespread in the west, also in California, Canada and south to Kansas and New Mexico.

The scientific name is *Shepherdia argentea.* It is a silvery shrub five to 20 feet tall, growing in draws or along water courses. The leaves are grey-green, silvery, and the branches are thorny.

These thorns make it a bit difficult to gather the fruit. Some people beat the bushes, first laying a canvas on the ground.

Not all the bushes bear fruit. Some bear pollen only. The fruit looks like a small orange-red currant, but it grows attached right to the branch and not on racemes like the currant. The taste is sour and, to some people, bitter.

There is one seed, about the size of a tomato seed.

The Indians ate the fruit raw or cooked it into a sauce which was used with buffalo meat — hence the name — or they dried a supply for winter use.

Some people believe the berries are edible only after a frost but I have eaten them before and they were fine.

Pectin is not needed for the jelly if the berries are picked before frost, when they are more acid. The jelly has a piquant taste, rather like currant, but the color is more golden. A preserve can be made using the whole fruit.

When extracting the juice, some people are upset to find that it has a milky appearance. One jellymaker canned the juice, then thought it had spoiled and threw it out. Boiling the juice with sugar does away with the milkiness, also the riper the berries, the less milkiness there is.

A related species *Shepherdia canadensis,* is called bitter buffaloberry or soapberry. The berries contain a high percentage of saponin, which not only gives them a bitter taste, but also allows them to be whipped like cream into a frothy dessert — if you can stand the taste. The Indians used them fresh and dried.

The flowers of both silver buffaloberry and bitter buffaloberry are small and inconspicuous. The family is Oleaster, which also contains Russian olive and silverberry (wolf-willow).

Kinnikinnick

Arctostaphylos uva-ursi

If you have used the bright red berries and shiny green leaves of kinnikinnick for holiday decorations, you are aware of one of the values of this common evergreen creeper.

It has many uses. The berries are edible and were used by the Indians and Eskimos. The berries are not very tasty, but in an emergency they could be boiled and eaten. They are a natural food for bears, rodents and birds. The name *uva-ursi* means bear's grape.

Kinnikinnick was used as tobacco by the Indians, sometimes mixed with real tobacco and sometimes mixed with the dried inner bark of red-osier dogwood.

In some parts of Sweden and Russia, the leaves, which contain tannin, are used for tanning hides.

Kinnikinnick is in the heath family, with the scientific name of *Arctostaphylos uva-ursi*. There are many species of *Arctostaphylos* found around the world.

Other common names are bearberry, hog cranberry, upland cranberry, and manzanita.

The plant grows in dry open woods, spreading a thick matted carpet. It helps prevent erosion because the roots hold sandy or gravelly soil.

The flowers which bloom in May and June are dainty wax-like pink and white jugs.

The leathery leaves are dried and used as tea in some parts of Russia, being known as Kutai or Caucasian tea.

It is not advisable to drink kinnikinnick tea unless you are very sure of the right proportion. Folk medicine books list the tea as a potent aid in chronic kidney disorders, but even there they advise against using the decoction pure.

Juniper

Common Juniper

Juniperus communis

What most people know about juniper is that the berries are used to flavor gin. The Indians used the berries as food but most of us would consider them food of the last resort. Juniper has a strongly resinous taste, both in the twigs and the fruit.

Junipers are evergreen shrubs or small trees. The leaves may be needle-like and prickly or scale-like. There are many species.

Rocky Mountain juniper *(J. scopulorum)* has both scale-like leaves and needle-like ones. It grows into a slender tree up to 30 feet tall.

Creeping juniper *(J. horizontalis)* is a spreading shrub less than a foot above the ground.

Common juniper *(J. communis)* is one of the most widely distributed woody plants in the world. Many cultivated forms of this juniper are planted as ornamental shrubs in gardens. It can be a tree or a low prostrate shrub. It has very sharp pointed needle-like leaves. The shrub form sometimes grows in large clumps, generally on north slopes and in open forests.

Juniper fruit is a hard berry, bluish-green with a white bloom. The berry is really a modified cone. If you look closely, you can make out on the surface two or more little points that correspond to the tips of cone scales.

The berries of the common juniper are the ones used to flavor gin. In olden times, the berries had many uses. American Indians dried them and stored them for winter. The flavor would be too strong for us today, but in those sparser-provisioned times, people ground the berries into a meal for mush or mealcakes.

In Sweden, during the old days, roasted juniper berries were used as a coffee substitute. In Germany, they were used to flavor sauerkraut. In France a kind of beer was made by fermenting a decoction of equal parts of juniper berries and barley. In England the ripe berries were used as a substitute for pepper.

Some of the Mexican junipers have berries that are much more palatable. They are quite large and have a sweetish pulp.

The oil of some juniper berries is used in medicines.

If you wish to try juniper berries, pick the fruit and try some raw and some cooked. The Indians ate the berries raw so it is possible.

However, eating them in quantity has caused irritation to the kidneys and upset digestion.

Juniper tea, made from either the berries or young twigs, is a better possibility. Some people actually like the strong pine-like taste. Others drink it because they say it is healthful. It does have a slight medicinal effect, namely as a diuretic.

The berries are ripe in the fall.

High-bush Cranberry

Viburnum trilobum

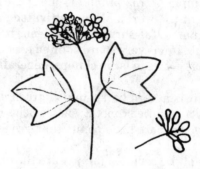

High-bush cranberry is entirely different from the ordinary cranberry we eat for Thanksgiving and Christmas.

The ordinary cranberry grows in a bog and is in the heath family, the same family as the huckleberry and the blueberry.

High-bush cranberry is in the honeysuckle family, in the *Viburnum* genus.

There are two or three *Viburnum* species called high-bush cranberry, some growing in the wild, some cultivated in gardens and parks.

The name high-bush cranberry came from the fact that the berries have been used as a substitute for ordinary cranberries. However, most people would agree, high-bush cranberries are a poor substitute. The fruit is bitter and acid. But in an emergency, this fruit could be a source of vitamin C, especially since the berries stay on the bush well into winter.

The European high-bush cranberry — *Viburnum opulus* — was known to be a health food as far back as Chaucer's time. Chaucer wrote that the guelder-rose (that is a common name) "shal be for your hele" and gave the advice, "picke him right as they grow and eat hem in."

Many people died of scurvy in those days and, if they had heeded Chaucer, they would have found a cure in their own backyard.

The American high-bush cranberry is *Viburnum trilobum*. It is an upright shrub three to 10 feet tall. The leaves, which are opposite and three-lobed, turn scarlet in the fall. The white flowers, blooming in May or June, are in a flat cluster.

The small bright scarlet berries have one large flat seed and soft pulp. After a frost, the fruit softens and has a slightly better flavor.

The fruit has been used for jelly, in pemmican, ground up into a relish, cooked into a meat sauce to serve with game, and as a tea.

A wild viburnum of the northwest is squashberry or mooseberry *(V. edule)*. It is similar to *V. trilobum* and is sometimes called the same common name, high-bush cranberry. The fruit is much less bitter and acid than *V. trilobum* or *V. opulus*.

The garden snowball is a variety of *V. opulus*. It has white flowers in a showy cluster but the flowers are sterile. They do not bear fruit.

Sunflower

Common Sunflower *(Helianthus annuus)*

Common sunflower can be a 15-foot garden plant with a single flower head as big as a dinner plate and it can be a wildflower growing only a few feet tall with many small flowers. It is the same *Helianthus annuus*.

It is a native American plant which was taken to Europe and there developed into the large-headed commercial variety that gives us the four-angled seeds we feed to birds and eat ourselves. In tribute to the European odyssey, the commercial variety is sometimes called Russian sunflower.

The wild sunflower has smaller seeds and the plant branches. The heads are never larger than three or four inches across.

The plant grows along roadsides and in waste places. The flowers are yellow with brown or purple centers and can be seen from June to September.

The stem is bristly and the leaves, which are ovate (egg-shaped), feel

139

like sandpaper.

Common sunflower is an annual. There are many sunflowers, some being annuals and some perennials. Two of the species, Jerusalem artichoke and Maximilian's sunflower, have tuberous roots which are edible.

The Indians made good use of the sunflowers, especially the seeds, which furnished flour and oil.

The seeds of wild sunflower are small compared to the cultivated variety but they can be used raw or roasted. The hull is quite thin. The Indians sometimes ate the roasted seeds hull and all.

Sunflower seeds, both wild and cultivated, are rich in oil. The Indians boiled the seeds until the oil was released and floated on top of the water. It was then skimmed off and used in cooking.

Today, sunflower oil is obtained commercially by pressing the seeds of the cultivated variety. The oil is used for salads and in cooking.

Sunflower seeds are an excellent food, very high in protein. They are high in calories too but the calories are not empty. Besides the protein, there is iron, calcium and vitamins A, B, D and E.

Compared to peanuts, which are also an excellent food, sunflower seeds have four times as much iron and six times as much thiamine. The protein content in the two foods is the same. It is phenomenally high — 25 per cent, almost as high as that of the famous soybean.

The protein in nuts, grains and seeds is not the same type as is found in meat and milk but if eaten in the right combinations, nuts, grains and seeds can take the place of part of the meat in our diet.

Wild sunflower is the state flower of Kansas and is sometimes called Kansas sunflower.

The scientific name *Helianthus* comes from the Greek words *helios* for sun and *anthos* for flower.

Acorn

Quercus (many species)

The acorn is not a favorite food by any means but it is a possibility. Indians of both the east and west coasts used the nuts widely, and in old-time Europe, the poor people, in times of famine, practically lived on them.

140

The reason for the relegation of acorns to survival-food status is their high tannin, or tannic acid, content which gives a bitter taste and can cause digestive upsets. In order to use acorns as food, the tannic acid has to be removed. It is soluble in water so it is removed by leaching.

One method the Indians used was to boil the nuts in a solution of lye obtained from hardwood ashes. A method used by a California tribe was to bury the nuts in boggy ground near cold springs. The nuts would swell and soften and turn black but they would keep for years. The taste was sweet because the tannin was leached out by the water.

Some acorns are bitterer than others. Those of the black oak group have more tannin than the white oak group. In fact, some of the white oak group are considered "sweet" and have been eaten unleached — raw, boiled or roasted.

Pigs have been fattened on acorns for centuries and in the wild, deer eat them.

The early Indians used acorns to thicken soup and make a mush.

As with other nuts, acorns have a good percentage of fat. Some eastern Indian tribes rendered oil from the acorns and then used the oil to flavor such foods as mush, pumpkins, squash, hominy and corn soup.

If you want to experiment, you could try acorn bread. It is heavy and dark-colored, but, if made properly, it has a sweet, rather nutty taste. You would probably use only part acorn meal and the rest cornmeal or wheat flour. You could also try griddle cakes or muffins.

To leach out the tannin, you can grind the dry raw nuts, put the meal into a bag and place the bag in a stream for as long as is necessary — eight hours, one day, maybe two days.

If you don't have a stream, you can punch holes in the bottom of a plastic bucket, place a folded cloth over the holes, then put the acorn meal into the bucket. If you hang the bucket over a faucet and open the faucet just enough to keep water trickling through the meal, you will remove the tannin.

Another method is to boil the acorns on the stove, changing the water whenever it gets brown. I don't recommend this method because it uses expensive fuel and the same result can be obtained using cold water.

I don't expect many people to use acorns as food today but we can hold on to the knowledge, remembering that there have been times when acorns were the "staff of life."

Mushrooms are Delectable Tidbits — If You learn Them Properly

Eating wild mushrooms is not recommended unless you are willing to 1) study and 2) follow the rules. Even then there is some hazard. People who have eaten mushrooms all their life sometimes poison themselves. There is always the risk that an odd mushroom is nestled in a clump of perfectly edible ones.

Mushroom hunting is a fine hobby and I do not wish to discourage anyone. But there are poisonous mushrooms.

There are also many edible ones and some are quite easy to identify. Hopefully the following rules will enable would-be hunters to take up this hobby in safety.

1. Do not eat any mushroom unless you are 100 per cent sure of the identification. Ninety-nine per cent is not good enough. It must be 100 per cent.

2. The easiest way to start learning about mushrooms is to take a course. If the course includes field trips you will be learning by the best method possible. An expert will show you where the edible mushrooms grow and what they look like in the ground. This is very important. Even experts cannot always identify a mushroom if you bring them a single specimen and you have forgotten where it grew and how it grew. You have to see new little specimens and big old specimens all together in the natural habitat.

143

3. You need some good books. Some books are very expensive, some are relatively inexpensive. You can look them over in a bookstore or ask an expert which book he would recommend. Most mushroom hunters own more than one book. The advantage is that you have several photographs or drawings to compare. Mushrooms do not always look alike. Even with several books, you often have difficulty in identification. Here is the advantage of taking a course. You can bring your mushrooms to the instructor and have him verify your judgment.

But you should do your homework first. It is not fair to teachers to have fifteen or twenty people come calling every weekend with bags full of mushrooms. It is up to us to study our books and learn all we can before we ring the expert's doorbell.

4. Start with one or two kinds. Students in my edible plants class sometimes bring in a paper sack with a dozen different kinds. They empty this load on my desk and say, "What are they?"

In all honesty, I have to say I don't know. There are thousands of mushrooms. Long ago I said to myself, am I going to learn ten mushrooms or am I going to learn two thousand? I am not a mycologist. I simply want to eat morels, shaggy manes, puffballs, and maybe one or two more. So, I say to my students, please don't pick all the mushrooms in the woods and bring them in. I don't know them. Let's concentrate on the few kinds that are edible and good and easy to identify. Those are the criteria for mushroom hunters, especially beginners. Start with the ones that are edible and good and easy to identify. For the other one thousand ninety-five species, just enjoy looking at them, enjoy comparing them with their pictures in the mushroom books, but leave them in the woods or field. Please don't bring gunnysacks full of them to your teacher.

5. Examine each mushroom one by one. Discard any that looks the least bit different from the rest. Remember — if you are not 100 per cent sure, you cannot eat it. There is always the danger that an odd mushroom is growing in the middle of your favorite hunting grounds, right where you have been picking for years.

6. There is a proper procedure to follow when cutting or digging mushrooms. First, carry a basket so you can keep the different species separate. You would not want to mix a possibly poisonous kind with your edible ones. Put each different kind in a separate paper bag or wax paper wrapping. Plastic bags are not used because mushrooms are delicate and start disintegrating.

Carrying a knife is handy both for digging and cutting. If you are taking home species for identification, you need to dig the base of the mushroom. If you are picking just one known species for your dinner, use the knife to separate the clean top and stalk from the dirt-covered base. There is no use carrying the dirt home.

You can also check for worms. Quite often mushrooms will look perfect but when you slice the stalk straight across, you will see the telltale pinholes that mean worms have worked their way up into the cap. Discard all wormy specimens.

7. Learn to make a spore print. If you are going to eat wild mushrooms, you must be willing to work. Actually, making a spore print is not hard. Simply cut the cap off the stem and lay the cap on a piece of white paper with the gills resting on the paper. Spores will fall out of the gills and dust the paper. You will be amazed at how much "dust" there will be on the paper. Now you can see the color of the spores and that will help you identify the mushroom. The poisonous Amanitas for instance have white spores while the edible meadow mushrooms have chocolate-brown spores.

8. Don't trust any so-called tests for poisonous mushrooms: a coin turning color, mice chewing on them, etc. You simply have to learn the edible ones. If you do not have the patience to learn them, the only thing to do is to buy your mushrooms in the supermarket. What is it I say to my students — "Don't poison yourself for forty cents. That's all a can of mushrooms costs in the supermarket."

If you find yourself saying, "This mushroom looks poisonous," or "This mushroom looks edible," head for your books immediately. You need review. Looks have nothing to do with edibility.

9. Eat sparingly of any new kind of mushroom until you know how you react. Some people cannot eat any kind of mushroom. Others can eat only a small amount. Some people can feast on one kind of mushroom but another kind leads to trouble. There are also times when you get a bad reaction from a kind of mushroom you have been eating for years. This might simply be a change in your own system.

Build-up can occur also. For instance, eating the same type of mushroom three days in a row can sometimes cause trouble.

10. Don't mix different species and cook them together. One type at a meal is enough. Mushrooms are not like carrots or potatoes.

The three types of mushrooms generally considered safe for beginners to pick are the morels, puffballs and shaggy manes.

The morels are spring mushrooms, found April to June. There are several species, all edible and very tasty. The only danger is, when you ask the question — as you should — are there any poisonous mushrooms that look anything like these — the answer is yes, there are.

The false morels can be confused with the true morels. However, learning the difference is not too difficult. The true morels, which are in the *Morchella* genus, all have a pitted head in the shape of a pine cone.

145

The false morels are in several genera: *Gyromitra, Helvella,* and others. Some are edible and some are poisonous. Eating them is not recommended for beginners.

False morels have two general characteristics. One is that the head is not pitted and ridged. It is convoluted like a brain or wrinkled and wavy. The second is that the head folds down over the stalk like a skirt.

In true morels, the head is fastened to the stalk with no skirt drooping down.

Both the head and the stalk of the true morels are eaten. The stalks are hollow and should be opened and examined for bugs.

Some of the morels are light brown, some are black, and some are almost white.

Morels are so delicious, you don't need a fancy recipe. You can saute them, which means fry them quickly in an open pan in a small amount of butter or margarine, or a mixture of butter and salad oil.

Mushrooms are 90 per cent water, so you cannot hope to fry them dry like bacon. Simply cook them over moderately high heat, shaking the pan frequently, for three to five minutes. If any juice gathers in the pan, that as the base for a cream sauce or soup.

Morels are easily preserved for future use, by drying. Thread them on a cord and hang in a warm place where there is air circulating. When they are thoroughly dry, store in an airtight container.

Shaggy mane *(Coprinus comatus)* is often found in huge quantities. It generally grows along roads, both paved and graveled, but I have seen it in grass in backyards.

It grows in clumps or groups. Mature mushrooms can be eight inches tall and look like closed shaggy umbrellas. When coming through the ground, the young mushrooms look like little white buttons. As they grow, they elongate into a cylinder with a shaggy skirt coming down over the stalk. The color is white with scattered yellowish-brown scales.

The shaggy mane does not last long, either on the stem or after being picked. It turns into black ink, starting at the edge of the skirt. If only the edges are black, you can cut them off and use the upper part.

The rapidity with which the shaggy mane disintegrates (the process is called autodigestion) is amazing. You can drive along a road one day and see both sides lined with clumps of mushrooms, then two days later, there is nothing there. If you look closely, you will see some black splotches. The mushrooms literally dissolved into black ink.

Shaggy manes must be cooked very quickly after picking as they will turn black even in the refrigerator.

They are excellent sauteed, creamed, made into soup or scrambled with eggs.

146

Look for them in summer and fall. Don't be afraid to pick all you want — all you can use anyway. Mushrooms come up from an underground mycelium which sends up new mushrooms year after year as long as there is a food supply and the right amount of moisture and warmth. New patches of mycelium are started by spores from mature mushrooms.

Puffballs are found from early spring to late fall. There are many kinds. The easiest to identify are those in the *Calvatia* genus because they are so big. They can be the size of a basketball and can weigh 20 pounds. They often grow in a bare field and from a distance look like white rocks. They have no gills and no stalks.

The important thing to remember about the smaller-sized puffballs — those the size of a golfball or baseball — is to cut them in half and look for the emerging gills and stem of the poisonous Amanitas. The Amanitas — like many mushrooms — come through the ground in a round button stage. The button can grow as large as a tennis ball before it opens into the toadstool shape. I myself have found button-stage Amanitas and thought they were puffballs until I cut them in half and saw the outlines of the gills and stem.

If you find a puffball as large as a basketball, there is no danger. There is nothing else it can be but a puffball. If it is old, it could be inedible. Puffballs should be white inside. They should have the color and consistency of cream cheese. If they are yellow or brown, they are too old to eat. Puffballs can be sliced and fried like eggplant. In fact, they can be used in almost any recipe that calls for eggplant: casseroles, stewed, baked with tomato and cheese, scrambled with eggs. One friend dices the puffball and uses it as a substitute for meat in meat loaf.

This mushroom is easy to dry or freeze. To dry, cut it in thin strips. To freeze, cut the size slices you want after defrosting.

The meadow mushrooms are harder to identify because they have gills. If you are going to start eating wild gilled mushrooms, you have to learn the poisonous Amanitas so that you won't make a mistake.

Any species of Amanita — and there are many — will have white gills and spores; it will have a cup at the base of the stem; and it will have a remnant of veiling on the stem. The color of the cap can vary from bright red to orange to buff to pure white.

The common names "destroying angel" and "death cap" will tell you how very poisonous these mushrooms are.

The shape of the Amanitas often closely resembles the classic "toadstool" picture of children's books. However, "toadstool" does not necessarily mean an Amanita. Today the word "toadstool" is used interchangeable with mushroom.

The cultivated mushroom, that you buy in stores, is one species of meadow mushroom. It is generally sold in the button stage. In the wild, you can find meadow mushrooms almost a foot across.

The genus of meadow mushrooms is *Agaricus*. There are many species. The identifying characteristics is chocolate brown spores and gills that turn chocolate brown at maturity. The gills in the young mushrooms are generally pink. The difficulty with identifying meadow mushrooms is that some species have gills that are almost white when young. The caps are usually white too. You can see how an unwary amateur could pick an *Amanita* by mistake. I would not start eating meadow mushrooms until I was past the amateur stage of mushroom hunting.

The fairy ring *(Marasmius oreades)* is another gilled mushroom that is edible and good. It is also easy to find because it grows in lawns in cities, making big circles that the homeowner tries to eradicate from his grass. The problem with fairy ring is that it it is not the only mushroom that grows in "fairy rings" in city lawns. If you want to eat *Marasmius oreades,* have an expert point out the differences between it and the following poisonous mushrooms: *Clitocybe dealbata, Panaeolus foenisecii,* and some of the *Entoloma* genus.

There are many edible mushrooms but the only ones I feel are safe for beginners are the morels, shaggy manes and puffballs. Even then the rules must be followed. Mushrooms are not for everyone and they are not for every day.

Scientifically, mushrooms are fungi. They don't contain chlorophyll and they don't manufacture their own food. Most are saprophytes, meaning they live on dead organic matter.

The vitamin and mineral content is low. The calorie content is also low, a fact which delights dieters until they start cooking the mushrooms in butter and cream and find they are adding all the calories the original food didn't have.

If you find more mushrooms than you can use fresh, you can experiment with freezing, drying and canning.

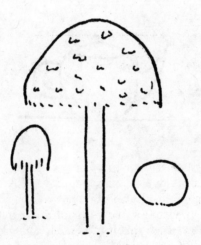

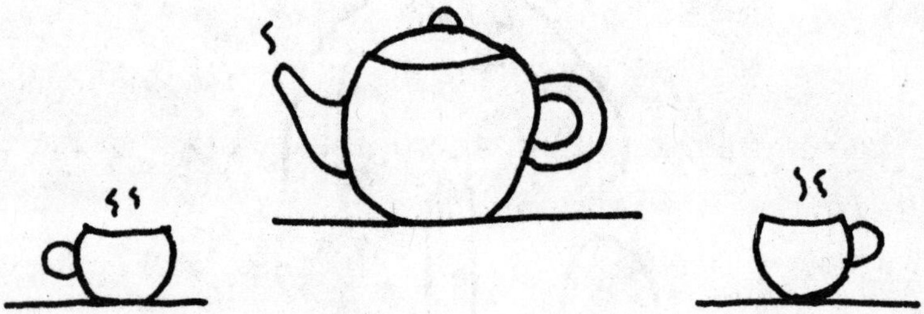

Herb Teas are Soothing and Free

You don't have to be seventy-two years old to enjoy herb tea. College students drink it, poker players drink it, office workers drink it.

Many people like to drink something hot but they don't want the caffeine that is in both coffee and Oriental tea. So they pour hot water on strawberry leaves, mint leaves, clover blossoms, pulverized rose hips.

Herb tea used to be a household standby. It went out of fashion but now it is making a comeback, along with the renewed interest in natural foods, backpacking, home gardens, and arts and crafts. People are interested in how our ancestors lived, what they ate and drank.

People drank hot beverages before Oriental tea was known. They drank different beverages afterwards too, sometimes for medicinal reasons, sometimes for the simple pleasure of a different taste.

The word tea comes from the tree that furnishes Oriental tea, *Thea sinensis,* now generally classified as *Camellia sinensis.*

Herb tea means an infusion made out of an herb. It does not have to be made out of a leaf. Rose hip tea is made out of the fruit of the rose.

Another word used for herb tea is tisane, which comes from the Latin *ptisane,* meaning peeled barley or barley water. People used to drink barley water.

There has always been a great deal of debate over the medicinal value of herb teas. Some people say the medicinal value is the non-drinking of coffee and tea. You are putting hot water in your stomach and that is soothing, warming and relaxing. Also the drinking of hot water in the company of others is a social occasion and that is relaxing.

However, there definitely are herbs that are medicinal and people make teas from them. Books on that subject are in the herb medicine category.

Since this book is about edible plants, I'll include only the herbs commonly used as a substitute for Oriental tea or coffee.

Many of these are medicinal in the sense that they have a high nutritive value and teas made from them have been used as a tonic. Today we know that the tonic effect is due to vitamins and minerals, especially vitamin C, the anti-scurvy vitamin.

If we can find wild plants that can be used for an herb tea that is pleasant to drink and also furnishes vitamin C, we are far ahead of the Oriental tea routine. We have new tastes to savor, the product is free, there is nutritive value but no caffeine, and when we are out camping, all we have to carry is the knowledge of which plant to put in the teapot.

I have already mentioned, in the individual plant descriptions, many which are used for tea. The seven I keep on hand in quantity are rose hip, mint, strawberry leaf, raspberry leaf, water-cress, clover and nettle.

Some people make mixtures such as clover and mint. Many wild teas are bland in flavor. If you are accustomed to drinking strong Oriental tea, you will probably find wild teas dull. You will also find them colorless. The color in Oriental tea comes from tannin. Most wild teas do not contain tannin.

Mint has a strong flavor and can be used to pep up blander teas.

Honey also helps. I like honey as the sweetener for wild teas. It enhances the flavor without overpowering it.

Proper drying and storing helps preserve the delicate flavor of the herbs, also the vitamin content.

I pick the herbs in spring or early summer and dry them indoors at room temperature. I do not use direct sun nor the oven. I feel the volatile oils, that are responsible for the flavor, are treated more gently by drying at room temperature. Some people put their herbs in paper bags and hang them from the ceiling. If your house does not lend itself to such an unconventional use, you can place the leaves on a wire rack on your counter or in a corner near your central heating system. An attic is good, if it is airy. You need a dry, airy, shady place.

Some people give their herbs a finishing touch in the oven. This is to remove the last bit of moisture. Then pack immediately in tightly closed containers. Light and moisture are bad for dried herbs, so the best storage is a sealed can. If you use glass jars, place them in a dark spot. If you use plastic bags, place the bag inside a can or use a brown paper sack inside the plastic sack. Herbs can lose their flavor rapidly and you will end up with blah teas.

Most herbs can be used fresh or dried. The vitamin C content of tea made from fresh strawberry leaves is high enough so that people in the old days dug the leaves from under snow in spring and made a spring tonic. Vitamin C is water soluble so an herb tea made from the leaves would be the equivalent of dissolving an ascorbic acid tablet in a cup of water.

Violet leaves, water-cress and nettle can all be used in the same way. If you do not wish to eat the greens, you can make an herb tea and drink the vitamin-rich essence.

Plants that are rich in vitamin C as the afore-mentioned will retain a considerable amount even if dried and stored.

Rose hips, which are the fruit of the rose, are so rich in vitamin C that they are used commercially. You can buy tablets and syrup made from rose hips in drugstores. The fruit is plentiful enough so you can pick all you want. Dry it at room temperature and store either whole or ground into powder. I like to think the vitamin content is better preserved if I store the hips whole and grind them with a mortar and pestle when I want to make tea.

Since the flavor of the rose hip tea is very mild, you can add cinnamon and clove, a mint leaf, or a curl of dried orange peel. There are few hard and fast rules for herb teas. You can make your own combinations.

Mint tea is a favorite with almost everyone. There are several kinds of mint: field mint, spearmint and peppermint. Peppermint is probably the best-flavored for herb tea. After you locate mint patches in the wild, you can cut and dry a good supply and you can also bring home a root and plant it in your garden so you can have fresh mint.

Bergamot is in the mint family but it is a larger coarser plant. Two species have been used for tea: the lavender-flowered *Monarda fistulosa,* also called horsemint, and the red-flowered *Monarda didyma,* American bee-balm, which grows wild in the east. That Monarda became known as Oswego tea because it was used by early Americans as a substitute for British tea. The Monardas do not make an especially palatable tea. They have a strong distinctive flavor and can cause stomach upset if brewed too strong or used very often.

On the other hand, you will find that some of the herb medicine books cite the Monardas as a cure for stomachache.

There are many plants that are in this category. They have been used as both medicine and as ordinary food or drink.

The famous chamomile, for instance, is drunk as a social-occasion tea but it has very specific medicinal qualities, and some people get a headache if they drink several cups or drink it several days in succession. The perennial chamomile is more potent than the annual. Three flowerheads to a cup of tea of the true Roman chamomile is all that is recommended.

There are several plants called chamomile and all are used for tea so you often do not know which plant you actually have in your tea mixture.

True chamomile is the Roman chamomile, *Anthemis nobilis,* a European plant grown commercially. Annual chamomile is *Matricaria Chamomilla* and it is also a cultivated plant.

The plant called pineapple weed, *Matricaria discoidea,* is common in the wild and is sometimes used for tea and is sometimes called chamomile but is not the genuine product.

Both the perennial and the annual chamomile are used as a calmative and a digestant. Herb tea made from them used to be given to teething babies to soothe them. Adults used it as a nervine and as a cure for indigestion.

Other plants of this halfway station between medicine and social teas are tansy, yarrow and mullein. They are all used for tea but I think they are potent and should not be used casually. Mullein is an ingredient of homemade cough syrups. Tansy and yarrow have been used in medicine since ancient times. I think we have so many other wild plants to choose from why use these potent medicinal herbs for a simple afternoon drink.

The only goldenrod really recommended for tea is an eastern species, *Solidago odora,* and even that one has resinous qualities. The western *Solidago missouriensis* has been used but no one recommends it for simple pleasure.

Western Labrador-tea, either *Ledum glandulosum* or *Ledum groenlandicum,* was used by the settlers but even they advised against using it too generously because it could have a laxative effect.

Sagebrush, *Artemisia tridentata,* has been used as a tea but it definitely is a medicinal tea, recommended for treating headache, stomachache and diarrhea.

The sage tea generally mentioned is made from the household chicken-stuffing herb, *Salvia oficinalis,* which is in the mint family.

Whether catnip tea is medicinal, is open to discussion. It has been used as a tranquilizer and as a home remedy for baby colic. The plant is *Nepeta cataria.*

Pine needle tea tastes like medicine and few people drink it, but in an emergency it could be an excellent source of vitamin C. Douglas fir needles can also be used. In fact, most of the conifers have been used for tea at one time or another.

There is one conifer that must be avoided: ground hemlock, *Taxus canadensis*. It is a toxic plant.

I have drunk tea made from Ponderosa pine. It's not too resinous if steeped for a short time only.

Old-timers often mention boiled tea. I think most of us would find boiled tea too strong. The generally accepted way to brew tea is to make an infusion, which means you pour boiling water on the leaves and let them steep, usually for five or 10 minutes. Very mild herbs can be steeped 15 minutes.

Dandelion and chicory roots are boiled but most people consider that beverage coffee and not tea. You can make tea out of both of these plants if you wish — using the leaves.

Some people like a bit of bitter dandelion taste along with the blandness of say, nettle tea or violet leaf tea. Roasted dandelion root will add color if you object to the pale color of most herb teas.

Nettle tea has often been used in Europe in times of emergency. German soldiers drank it as their regular beverage when there was no coffee or Oriental tea available.

New Jersey tea, *Ceanothus americanus*, is used in eastern U.S. It was drunk by George Washington's soldiers.

Sassafras, *Sassafras albidum,* is both a beverage and home remedy. It is also an ingredient in some recipes for root beer.

Wintergreen, *Gaultheria procumbens,* which can also be used in root beer, makes a good herb tea. Both the leaves and the red berries are used. The flavor is wintergreen as the name tells you.

Some other plants you might want to try, either alone or in combinations, are alfalfa, plantain and shepherd's purse.

There are some wild teas that are more like lemonade or a fruit juice drink. Sumac tea, for instance, is often called lemonade or even "Rhus-jhus."

And what do you have if you steep dried elderberries or chokecherries and make a spicy drink for a cold winter evening?

Perhaps it does not matter what you call your beverage. If it's hot and satisfying, that's all that matters.

I say, make your cup, take it to a restful spot and meditate where it came from. Not from China but from the picnic you went on last August where the sun was bright and the shade was deep and you had a lovely day and this is what you brought home — the memory of a lovely day and a handful of herbs to dry for winter teas.

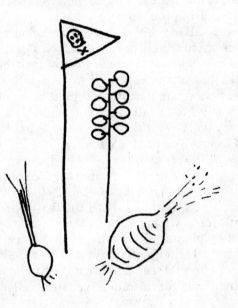

Beware of These Poisonous Plants

The best advice on avoiding poisonous plants is to eat nothing wild unless you are 100 per cent sure of your identification.

If you do eat something that you suspect is poisonous, rush to a doctor, taking along a sample of what you ate. If you are out of reach of a doctor, try to make yourself vomit.

In cases of mild stomach upsets, drinking milk often eases the discomfort.

The word poisonous does not necessarily mean deadly poisonous. Some plants kill people and animals. Others have toxic qualities and will cause illness but not a fatal illness. A third category of toxicity might be termed simply discomfort or stomach upset.

If you follow the rules for eating any wild food, you will avoid the poisonous ones.

There are some folk-tale bits of advice that may lead you astray. For instance, some people say "I eat what the birds eat." You can go very wrong on that. Birds eat both poison ivy and baneberry fruit with evidently no ill effects. Animals can eat certain toxic plants also.

Another idea you might have is that cooking will destroy the toxic substances. In some cases, this does work. Cooking the berries of black nightshade *(Solanum nigrum)* seems to render them non-toxic to most people. But in other plants, the toxic substances are unchanged by heat.

Milky juice sometimes denotes a poisonous plant — dogbane, for instance — but other plants with milky juice — salsify and dandelion, for instance — are edible.

Some plants are on the borderline of being edible or toxic. They are included in both poisonous and edible listings. This is because a little is okay but too much can have bad effects. For instance, curly dock and sheep sorrel are sometimes listed as toxic. It seems that a large quantity of soluble oxalates in your system can interfere with calcium

157

absorption. Spinach is in this category too.

And, of course, there are all the plants that are edible at only a certain time of year or have one part of the plant edible and another toxic, such as elderberry, where the ripe fruit is edible and good while the leaves and stems are toxic.

The worst piece of advice you can follow is "It looks edible." Plants can look delicious and you can still get poisoned.

The only way to be safe is to eat nothing that you can not positively identify.

Learning the common poisonous plants of the area will help in identifying the edible ones.

Death-camas

Zigadenus venenosus

Death-camas is one of the reasons people who eat wild foods have to be careful when they go out and start digging.

The bulb and the new spring growth of death-camas looks like the bulb and new spring growth of the edible blue camas. The flowers are different so if you wait until the blossoms are out, you can tell them apart.

The two are different genera. Blue camas is *Camassia quamash.* Death-camas is the *Zigadenus* genus and there are three main species, all containing harmful ingredients.

The flowers of *Zigadenus* are white or greenish-white while the flowers of *Camassia quamash* are blue, but the shape is quite similar — six petals (actually three sepals and three petals) and six stamens.

Zigadenus venenosus has two varieties but they look much alike and they are, as the name suggests, very poisonous.

The flowers are cream colored, small, and arranged in a compact raceme.

This species, called meadow death-camas or deadly zigadenus, is very common and can be a serious hazard to cattle and sheep because the bright green leaves come out in early spring before there is much other grazing.

Zigadenus paniculatus, panicled death-camas, has the flowers in a longer raceme.

Zigadenus elegans, called wand-lily or mountain death-camas, has fewer blossoms but they are large enough to be distinct up and down the stalk rather than in a cluster.

The leaves of all the *Zigadenus* are grasslike. The flowering stalk varies from less than a foot to two feet high. Some of the species grow in dry soil, some in wet meadows and some in alpine zones. Flowering season is June to August.

The poisonous substance is alkaloids and you need very little to get fatal results.

One of the common names attached to *Zigadenus* is poison sego, which suggests how easy it is to confuse the bulb of death-camas with edible bulbs such as sego lily. Other names for death-camas are white camas and poison camas.

It is said even the Indians were sometimes poisoned by *Zigadenus.* You can see where the difficulty would be if you were digging bulbs in early spring before the flowers were out or in late summer after the blooms had died, and you were trying to gather sego lily, blue camas, wild onion, fritillary, wild hyacinths — all of which are edible — but in among them might be growing a misplaced death-camas.

When Lewis and Clark chose to buy their root supplies from the Indians instead of digging for them, they were probably avoiding more than the work of spading the ground.

False Hellebore

Veratrum viride

False hellebore sometimes tempts early spring campers into trouble because this poisonous plant sends up its first little shoots with leaves tightly rolled, looking like a rather luscious sprout.

A lesson for all experimenters in edible wild foods is to eat nothing until you can identify it exactly and that means in all stages of growth — new shoots, flowering plant and seed stage.

You cannot go by common names. You must use the full botanical name.

Hellebore, for instance, is very confusing. There is a plant called hellebore which we grow in our gardens. It is the true hellebore — *Helleborus niger* or Christmas rose and it is in the buttercup family. False hellebore is *Veratrum viride* of the lily family.

Sometimes *Veratrum viride* is called skunk cabbage and that is bad because the true skunk cabbage has roots that have been eaten by people after roasting but false hellebore must never be eaten.

The false hellebore plant looks entirely different from skunk cabbage as soon as the leaves start to unroll. *Veratrum* grows three to six feet tall — cornstalk-style — but coarse and with large leaves. The leaves have a pleated look due to the well-marked parallel veins.

The yellowish-green flowers are in a large loose spike at the top of the stalk. The lower branches of this flower spike tend to droop.

Another *Veratrum* is *V. californicum* — also poisonous — which looks much like *V. viride* but it is a larger plant with white flowers and the entire flower spike stands erect.

Both *Veratrums* are called false hellebore, skunk cabbage, and sometimes cornlily. But the names green false hellebore and American false hellebore are generally reserved for *V. viride. Viride* means green.

If you hear the name Indian poke attached to *V. viride,* be careful that you don't associate it with the edible pokeweed or poke which is *Phytolacca americana.*

The *Veratrums* are poisonous to both humans and livestock. The flowers are even poisonous, as has been proven by the death of honeybees.

The Indians used *Veratrum* as medicine — it lowers blood pressure — but they knew the plant well because it is said they also used it to commit suicide.

Animals generally avoid it, probably because it has a burning taste.

Veratrum grows in moist areas — wet meadows, along streams and in low woods. The first shoots come up soon after the snow departs. Flowers are in bloom June to August.

Poison Ivy

Rhus radicans

Poison ivy is a plant most people learn to recognize early in life, sometimes because they have had a bout of the rash and blisters caused by contact with the plant's poisonous oil.

The plant can be either a vine which is the common eastern form or a low shrub which is the common Rocky Mountain form. The scientific name *Rhus radicans* refers to both forms and the name poison ivy refers to both. The name poison oak can refer to both also but there is a different species, *Rhus diversiloba,* growing mostly in the Pacific Coast area, which has oakleaf-shaped leaflets and is generally called poison oak, although the name poison ivy can be used.

Both forms of *Rhus radicans* have shiny green leaves made up of three leaflets, more or less notched at the edges. The flowers are small and greenish and grow in clusters. The fruit is clusters of smooth whitish berries.

The leaves turn red and orange in autumn. The berries keep their white color.

The berries are poisonous to humans but birds eat them. This proves we cannot listen to people who say you can eat any berries birds and animals eat.

The poisonous oil can be easily spread, which means you can get blisters by coming near a brushfire which is burning the plant. You can get the oil on your skin by touching your shoes or some one else's shoes.

If you do get the oil on your skin, wash immediately with strong soap and water. To relieve the itching, some people use strong tea, others use household ammonia or a commercial product.

The oil can get in your eyes and cause severe complications.

Poison ivy belongs in the sumac family. Some of the sumacs have edible berries. You can make a "pink lemonade" from the fruit of staghorn sumac, smooth sumac and squawbush.

The cashew nut is in the sumac family. When raw, the nut is poisonous but roasting destroys the poison.

Water-hemlock

Cicuta douglasii

You can poison yourself with water-hemlock. That is the reason people have to be very careful when digging any wild roots to eat. There are many edible plants in the parsley family — where water-hemlock belongs — but there are also some very poisonous ones.

Water-hemlock, *Cicuta douglasii,* is said to be the most poisonous plant in the north temperate zone. One good-sized bite is enough to kill a person. John Hughes, originator of the Hughes Gardens in Missoula, is said to have died of eating water-hemlock. While working his land, he unearthed what he thought were "root artichokes" and he ate a couple of bites.

162

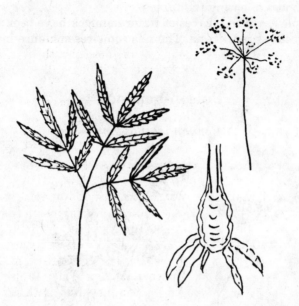

This is a lesson to all of us wild-food eaters: do not even taste anything you are not 100 per cent sure of.

Water-hemlock is a sturdy perennial with thick rootstocks looking like tubers. The stems are two to seven feet tall with compound leaves divided into saw-toothed leaflets. The white flowers, which bloom June through August, are in an umbel of the type found in Queen Anne's lace and other members of the parsley family.

The plant grows on wet ground in both low valleys and high mountains.

To identify water-hemlock, you have two distinguishing characteristics. One is that the leaf veins end, not at the tips of the teeth, but in the notches between the teeth. Secondly, in the older plants, the part of the stem that is underground, close to the bundle of thickened roots, is filled with horizontal partitions.

There is another species of *Cicuta, C. bulbifera,* which is a smaller plant and has tiny bulbs in the leaf axils.

Water-hemlock is sometimes called cowbane (very appropriate as cows have died from eating the tubers) and also poison-hemlock. However, the true poison-hemlock, which is the plant that killed Socrates, is *Conium maculatum,* also a member of the parsley family and also deadly.

The poison in *Cicuta,* cicutoxin, affects the respiratory system, causing convulsions followed by a rather quick death. Mr. Hughes died within two hours of eating the tubers.

Some people say dried leaves of water-hemlock have been at times mistakenly sold as marijuana. There is some resemblance in the leaf structure.

Poison-hemlock

Conium maculatum

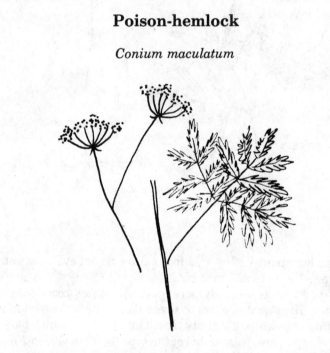

Poison-hemlock is the plant that killed Socrates. It is a close relative of the equally poisonous water-hemlock. Both are in the parsley family — the *Umbelliferae* — which contains many edible plants (parsley, carrot, parsnip, the wild biscuit-root, yampah) but it also contains many poisonous ones.

Poison-hemlock has the general look of wild carrot (Queen Anne's lace) but it is a larger plant — two to eight feet tall — and is much branched.

The stems are hollow, grooved and spotted with purple. If you crush the stems, you get an unpleasant odor. The finely divided leaves are dark green and can be a foot long.

The small white flowers are in umbrella-like clusters called umbels. They bloom June to August.

The plant is native to Eurasia but by now it is found all over the world. It grows in damp places along ditches and roadsides, in hedges, open woods and waste places.

The fruit is small, egg-shaped and has wavy ribs. It is greyish-brown in color.

All parts of the plant are poisonous. The poison paralyzes the respiratory system.

The scientific name is *Conium maculatum*. Other common names are spotted hemlock and poison parsley.

Poison-hemlock can be confused with other members of the parsley family. There are many plants that grow in the manner of Queen Anne's lace.

People who eat wild plants have to be very careful with the parsley family.

Larkspur

Little Larkspur *(Delphinium bicolor)*

Little larkspur is not known to have poisoned people but it has killed livestock. It is in the buttercup family, the same family as the poisonous monkshood and baneberry.

The scientific name of larkspur is *Delphinium*. The garden larkspurs and delphiniums are in this genus also.

There are about 20 species of *Delphinium* in the U.S., some tall, some short, and all toxic in varying degrees.

D. bicolor is a low-growing species. It is especially prevalent in the northern Rockies. It is very similar to another low-growing larkspur, *D. nuttallianum,* commonly called low larkspur or Nelson's larkspur. The color of both species is a rich purple or deep blue.

The plants vary in height from six inches to two feet. There is one flowering stalk and a clump of leaves at the base. The leaves are finely cut and dissected.

The plants grow in open range and foothills and are grazed by cattle, with often dire results. In some areas, larkspur kills more cattle than the locoweeds.

The poison comes from alkaloids, one of which is called delphinine and has been used in medicine.

The most toxic stage is the early spring growth and that is exactly when cattle are hungry for new grass.

Domestic sheep are not affected by the poison. They are actually employed as a means of eradicating the plant. Elk eat the plant in late summer and fall when the toxicity has disappeared.

The name larkspur is a descriptive phrase which refers to the one prolonged sepal which can be compared to the spur on the foot of a bird.

Monkshood

Aconitum columbianum

Monkshood is a poisonous plant and cattle have died from eating it when other forage was scarce. It has also caused death to humans.

It is a stately plant, growing to six feet tall, with odd helmet-shaped flowers that are well described by the name monkshood. The hood or helmet is one enlarged sepal that rises over the others like a hood. The name originated in Europe, along with some other equally descriptive names: Odin's helm, Thor's hat, troll's hat.

The German name "devil's-root" refers to the poisonous quality of the roots. Actually, the whole plant is dangerous. There is a yellow-flowered monkshood in Asia that earned the name wolfsbane because wolf hunters used the juice of the root to poison the animals.

The monkshood of the Rockies is *Aconitum columbianum.* The flowers, which grow in slender spikes, can be a rich purple, greenish-yellow or a mixture of all these colors.

The leaves are alternate and palmately lobed — like the fingers on your hand.

Monkshood is in the buttercup family. This family contains other poisonous members, two of which are larkspur and baneberry.

European monkshood, *A. napellus,* furnishes the drug aconite. Sometimes the plant is referred to as aconite.

Many species of monkshood are grown in gardens and are handsome plants but it is wise to be aware of the poisonous qualities.

Monkshood is a perennial. It prefers a moist location and partial shade. It blooms in summer.

Baneberry

Actaea rubra

Baneberry has lovely shiny berries, either scarlet-red or milk-white, but do not be tempted. They are poisonous.

The berry is in a raceme and is quite conspicuous. It is rather beautiful, in fact. One of the names of the white-berried variety is chinaberry because the white fruit looks as if it were made of china.

Baneberry is a perennial one to three feet tall with a stout stem and thin lacy leaves.

The small white flowers are not showy. They appear in racemes May to July. The fruit ripens in summer, and is often still on the plants when blueberries are ripe, so children have to be warned. Baneberry can grow in the same habitat as blueberry, although it prefers a moister soil, especially shaded areas along streams.

The poison is an essential oil which causes severe gastroenteritis. The

167

Indians used the rootstock as a laxative, but we would call that living dangerously.

Baneberry is one of the fruits that proves you can not eat something just because birds and animals eat it. Birds seem to be able to eat the berries without ill effect.

Western Blue Flag

Iris missouriensis

To see a clump of iris out in the middle of a pasture makes you think, "Surely this plant escaped from someone's garden." Some plants do that. They escape from a garden and start families in the wild.

But western blue flag is a native, found in the west from Canada south to New Mexico, Arizona and California. It is smaller than most cultivated iris but it can be two feet tall. The flowers are pale violet-blue, sometimes so pale they seem white.

The plant blossoms May through July, in open wet fields and mountain valleys up to 9,000 feet.

Iris means rainbow and legend has it the flower was named after Juno's waiting-maid Iris, who later became the rain goddess. She wore a colorful robe that symbolized the rainbow.

From this legend, you can see how old a flower iris is. It was grown in Asia and Europe in ancient times. Look at the names of our garden iris: Siberian iris, Japanese iris, Persian iris.

There are about 150 species. Thirty are found in the U.S. Only one is in the Rockies.

We list iris under poisonous plants. There is a very bitter resinous substance called irisin in the rootstock and this substance can poison livestock. It can poison people too. It is said the Indians dipped their arrows in a poison made by grinding the roots of *Iris missouriensis* (meaning of Missouri), mixing with animal bile, putting it all in a gall bladder and warming it near a fire for several days.

Yet, in other sources, we read the Indians esteemed the rootstock of iris as a laxative and liver stimulant. This no doubt means that a little is very good, but a lot will kill you.

An iris that grows in southern Europe, Florentine iris, produces a valuable perfume called orris. The root is powdered and today it is used to scent soap and tooth powders. It has a violet odor. But in the Middle Ages, it was absolutely indispensable, not only in perfume but in the linen closets. No doubt many people can remember little silk packets smelling like violet in grandmother's linen closet. In Colonial days, the powdered hair was dusted with imported "violet powder" and that was the orris-root perfume.

Flag is a common name for iris. Western blue flag is also called Rocky Mountain iris.

Henbane

Hyoscyamus niger

Henbane is a poisonous plant that can lead people into trouble because the dried seed stalks are interesting and people bring them home for dried arrangements. The vase-shaped seed capsules are full of tiny seeds — like poppy seeds — and children could be tempted.

The plant is a coarse weedy herb that grows one to three feet high along roadsides and in dry waste places. It is sticky and clammy to the touch, with a strong unpleasant smell. The leaves are lobed and stalkless.

The flowers grow in a spike and are funnel-shaped, only an inch long, but quite showy. They are a mixture of greenish-yellow and purplish-yellow with dark purple veins. Blooming season is May through July.

The dry seed capsules are tiny perfectly-shaped urns fluted into five sharp points.

Henbane came from Europe where it was known since ancient times as both a medicinal drug and a poison.

It is grown commercially today in many countries, including the U.S. The dried leaves yield the drugs atropine, hyoscyamine and scopolamine, which are used for nervous disorders.

The plant is used in some parts of the world in its natural state as a narcotic drug. The dried leaves are steeped into a tea or smoked. This is living dangerously. Insane-root is one of the common names of the plant. Some people say henbane is the herb Shakespeare was referring to when Banquo asks, "Or have we eaten on the insane root that takes the reason prisoner?"

Many plants are in the category of being a medicine in some cases and a poison in others. Henbane was once used, for instance, to ease toothache, but it was too dangerous a remedy and the use was stopped.

The botanical name *Hyoscyamus niger* means black hogbean. An old book says "Swine having fed thereon, are much disturbed thereby, yea are in danger of their lives, if they wallow not themselves in water presently thereupon; neither do they go into the water to washe themselves, but to seeke after Crevises (crayfish), by the eating of which they recover."

The word henbane implies that hens would also be "much disturbed thereby."

People have been poisoned by eating the seeds.

The family is the *Solanaceae* — potato or nightshade — which includes several poisonous plants: black nightshade, belladonna, jimson-weed.

It also includes the potato, tomato and eggplant, which we eat with relish.

Animals generally avoid henbane because of its nauseous odor and taste.

Jimson-weed

Datura stramonium

A family was poisoned by eating a tomato grown on a jimson-weed plant. A man in Tennessee grafted a tomato plant on a jimson-weed plant, knowing they were both in the same family, and figuring he would get ripe tomatoes late in the fall because jimson-weed does not freeze off as early as tomato. He got the ripe tomatoes but he also got poisoned.

171

Jimson-weed is *Datura stramonium* and it is a common weed growing throughout North America along roadsides, in fields and waste places. It is a large annual, as tall as five feet, with a green or purplish stem, large coarse short-stalked leaves and funnel-shaped flowers that vary in color from white to bluish-purple. The fruit is a dry prickly capsule.

The leaves have a strong odor that is rather sickening. It is so strong it protects animals from being tempted to eat it. The plant can grow in hog pastures and the hogs won't eat it.

The name jimson-weed is a corruption of Jamestown-weed and that name came from the early association of the Virginia settlers with the plant. It seems some colonists tried to eat the leaves like spinach. According to a written account, "the Effect was a very pleasant Comedy; for they turn'd natural Fools for several Days..."

This plant is called in Spanish *yerba del diablo* — devil's weed — and it has been known for centuries for its hallucinogenic (meaning you see things that aren't there) powers.

Among the Indians of the southwest, the plant is used in witch-doctor *(diablero)* ceremonies. The effect is rather like that of using peyote or certain mushrooms.

The anthropologist Carlos Castaneda, during his studies in the southwest, was initiated by a *diablero* and part of the ceremony was to drink a concoction made from jimson-weed root. Castaneda wrote later the concoction smelled like cockroaches. After he drank it, he broke into a sweat, got stomach cramps, and waves of nervousness swept over him so his teeth chattered. Finally, he fell asleep and slept for two days.

This was voluntary but the family in Tennessee who ate the tomato grown on a jimson-weed graft had no idea what was going on. It took a lot of work by many doctors to trace the symptoms to the tomato. No one died, but two members of the family required hospitalization.

The seeds are very poisonous. Children can die from eating them.

Other common names of the plant are stinkweed, devil's trumpet, thornapple and mad apple.

Some Daturas are used as ornamentals in gardens. In Florida and California, you sometimes see the perennial angel trumpet which is an import from the Andes of Peru and is a small tree with very large white trumpet flowers.

The poisonous plant belladonna or deadly nightshade is in the same *Solanaceae* family and contains the same type of poisonous alkaloids. Many of these plants have medicinal uses. Belladonna contains the drug atropine, and jimson-weed has been used for thousands of years to alleviate asthma. But in the hands of unknowing people, the effect is generally just plain poisoning.

Climbing Nightshade

Solanum dulcamara

Climbing nightshade is an illustration of why you must use scientific names for plant identification. This plant is often called bittersweet but there is an entirely different plant called the same name. Sometimes a differentiation is made by calling climbing nightshade *(Solanum dulcamara)* European bittersweet and the other plant *(Celastrus scandens)* American bittersweet.

Both plants are vines but climbing nightshade has ruby-red berries while American bittersweet has two-tone berries, half red and half orange.

Climbing nightshade is a weak, trailing plant that can grow six or eight feet long, through hedges and over thickets. The leaves have two small lobes at the base. The flowers are purple and wheel-shaped, much like the flowers of potatoes or tomatoes.

The fruit is drooping clusters of shiny berries which are green at first and then turn red.

You can often find flowers and fruit on the vine at the same time.

The plant is poisonous to both animals and people. With people, it is the berries which tempt children.

There are other species of nightshade, all containing the same poisonous alkaloids that *S. dulcamara* has. Nevertheless, one of the nightshades is listed among edible plants. This is *S. nigrum,* black nightshade, also called common nightshade or garden nightshade. It is an annual, growing as a weed in waste places, height varying from one to three feet. The flowers are white and the fruit is black.

The ripe berries have been made into pies and preserves and some people have never had any ill effects. Luther Burbank developed a cultivated form which is grown in gardens under the name of wonderberry or garden huckleberry. The amount of alkaloids can vary with different soils and climates. Also, people vary in their reaction. If you want to experiment with black nightshade, you might try just a few berries — very ripe and well cooked.

Do not try the red berries of *S. dulcamara* at all.

The name deadly nightshade refers to another member of the *Solanaceae* family, *Atropa belladonna*. It is definitely poisonous.

The edible potato, tomato and eggplant are all in the *Solanaceae* family and there are some of the same poisonous alkaloids in the plants. Livestock has been poisoned by eating the vines, also by eating greened potatoes.

Dogbane

Apocynum androsaemifolium

Dogbane is not deadly poisonous but the name comes from the Greek for dog and away from, meaning dogs stay away from this plant.

Like many poisonous plants, dogbane has been used in medicine. Some tribes of Indians removed the green fruit from the pods, boiled it and drank the resulting liquid as a heart medicine.

The bitter root has been used as a laxative. I would not recommend it. Just the milky juice is enough to blister some people's skin.

There are several dogbanes. The common one is spreading dogbane, *Apocynum androsaemifolium,* which is also called flytrap dogbane because flies, searching for nectar, get stuck in the bell-shaped flowers.

You can spot the low shrub-like plant on dry hillsides, usually close to the edge of woods.

It grows about two feet tall, with forked, reddish branches and smooth ovate leaves that are paired. The leaves are slightly hairy underneath and both leaves and stem have a milky juice.

The flowers are small, pink or white, fragrant, and they hang at the ends of the branches.

Another plant in the dogbane genus is *A. cannabinum,* hemp dogbane or Indian hemp. It grows taller and the fibers were used by the Indians for making twine.

People who eat milkweed have to be careful not to confuse it with dogbane. Both plants have milky juice and leaves that grow opposite. The leaves of dogbane are narrower and the flowers are smaller.

Locoweed

Astragalus purshii

Locoweed is the plant animals eat and go loco. Actually, there are many different plants called locoweed. Most are in the *Astragalus* genus but some botanists call the crazyweed genus, *Oxytropis,* by the common name of locoweed also.

All these plants are in the pea family and are very difficult to tell apart. There are about 100 species of *Astragalus* in the U.S. and about 10 *Oxytropis.* Both *Astragalus* and *Oxytropis* have pea-like flowers and compound leaves — like climbing vetch, except that climbing vetch has tendrils and the other two don't.

Astragalus has three other common names besides locoweed: milk-vetch, poison-vetch, and rattle-pod.

A common locoweed of the Rockies is *Astragalus purshii.* Also called woolly-pod milkvetch, it has short, thick woolly seed pods. The plant is low-growing, about six inches tall, with prostrate gray foliage growing in tufts and white or purple flowers.

Not all of the *Astragalus* species are poisonous. Some are excellent feed for sheep, others have been used by the Indians for food — namely, the pods in soup.

The livestock poisoning caused by certain species of *Astragalus* is due sometimes to an alkaloid in the plants and sometimes to the selenium the plants absorb from certain shale soils.

Animals that eat selenium-rich plants become afflicted with "blind staggers." This is a nervous disorder, starting with "loco" behavior and ending in death.

Most animals do not eat the locoweeds if there is better range available but once they start, they become addicted and crave it. Sheep seem to be more susceptible to eating poisonous locoweeds. In the two summers of 1907 and 1908, about 15,000 sheep died in Wyoming.

Selenium is generally found in nature in very dilute amounts but the locoweeds act like a wick, pulling in the element until the concentration is very high.

The locoweeds grow in dry soil and bloom in late spring.

Index